CW01457561

The Lord of the Sabbath
The riches of God's rest

DayOne

© Day One Publications 2007
First printed 2007

ISBN 978-1-84625-068-2

9 781846 250682 >

ISBN 978-1-84625-068-2

All Scripture quotations, unless otherwise indicated, are taken from the **New King James Version**®, © 1982 by Thomas Nelson, Inc. Used by permission. All rights reserved.

British Library Cataloguing in Publication Data available

Published by Day One Publications
Ryelands Road, Leominster, HR6 8NZ
☎ 01568 613 740   FAX 01568 611 473
email—sales@dayone.co.uk
web site—www.dayone.co.uk
North American—email—sales@dayonebookstore.com
North American web site—www.dayonebookstore.com

Cover designed by Bradley Goodwin and printed by Gutenberg Press, Malta

Dedication

To Andrew

Contents

Acknowledgements

Without the combining of several factors this book would never have been written. I was privileged more than I realised at the time to be nurtured as a new Christian in an environment where the Bible was taken seriously, expounded carefully and applied faithfully with the reverence that the Word of God deserves.

Over the years the pummelling of these foundations from all angles has only served to demonstrate how indestructible they are. Some of the fiercest challenges in recent times have come from those who have sought to reinterpret the biblical teaching on the Sabbath and the law. Ironically, I am obliged to acknowledge that they have rendered me an invaluable service by directing me to diligent study in order to be sure as to what the Bible really says about these things.

From time to time circumstances arose which led to the need to expound passages of the Bible relating to the Sabbath. Because of the help this proved to be to a number of people and because of the way various erroneous views were highlighted in the process, I found myself increasingly under compulsion to set things out in order and try to present the biblical teaching in a systematic fashion which might benefit those looking for clarification in this area.

The friends who have encouraged me in this task and offered objective criticism know who they are, and I am greatly indebted to them. My wife, Rhiannon, has been a faithful helper and uncompromising critic as I have bounced my thoughts off her to see how they come back, and as she has carefully studied the manuscript.

Above all, I wish publicly to acknowledge the Lord whose grace has abounded toward me in the course of my study of this subject. For although I have come to understand more clearly than ever before that I do not keep the Fourth Commandment very well, rarely have I been so conscious of his presence as when I have been absorbed in a consideration of the Sabbath which was made for man, or longed more for that Day when full fellowship with him will be restored.

Keith Weber
January 2007

The idea of one day in seven being set apart has been with us from the creation of the world. The Hebrew practice of resting on the seventh day influenced all the surrounding nations. Josephus said: 'There is not any city of the Grecians, not any of the barbarians, nor any nation whatever, whither our custom of resting on the Sabbath day has not come'; and Philo: 'For that day is the festival, not of one country, but of all the earth' (Robert Cox, *The Literature of the Sabbath*, volume 1, page 116).

Generally speaking, by the time of the fourth century the day of rest had changed from the seventh day to the first day of the week, called the Lord's Day, which custom has prevailed in nations influenced by Christianity ever since. This is a subject which is described in Scripture from creation in Genesis to the day when the Holy Spirit moved to complete the canon of Scripture (Revelation 1:10). The way this is expressed in Revelation 1:10 is in itself a confirmation of biblical teaching about the Lord's Day. An adjective describes the day. It is 'the Lordly day' (τῇ κυριακῇ ἡμέρᾳ). This day belongs to the Lord who himself is Lord of the Sabbath.

There are features which have their origin in the Bible which have contributed to make Great Britain a great nation. As these features go into decline so the nation goes into decline. We see this especially in the creation ordinances of marriage and the family and the Sabbath. That Christians care about recovering biblical teaching is encouraging. This book is a sign of care.

Sports, consumerism and preference for leisure activities have eroded the Lord's Day. Few now take the Christian Sabbath to mean a whole day set apart. Neglect has been largely due to erroneous thinking or ignorance about what the Bible teaches. Jesus said the Sabbath was made for mankind's benefit (see chapter 6). This clear, constructive exposition is designed to establish and strengthen the Lord's Day for God's glory and our good. I heartily commend it.

Erroll Hulse
January 2007

Introduction

This book was born out of controversy—controversy among Christians. Yet it is not intended to be controversial. Stated perhaps over-simply, at one end of the controversy there are those who equate 'the Sabbath' with 'the Lord's Day' and maintain that the stipulations of the Fourth Commandment (Exodus 20:8-11) still apply to all people, while at the other there are those who argue that the Ten Commandments are in effect superseded in Christ and that in particular the fourth was essentially Jewish and therefore has no relevance to the Christian church, let alone to anyone else.

However, as a gentle caution to those who love an argument, this book is not an attempt to defend one position against another, but rather has been written out of a desire to examine what the Bible really says on the subject.

The trouble today in much of the Christian church is not controversy over the meaning of God's Word, but comfortable indifference. It is not that Christians have wrestled with these things and some have come down on one side of the argument while others have adopted the opposite viewpoint. Far from it. The problem is that such is the state of the church that most are not even aware that a problem exists. It is time to issue a wake-up call to those slumbering and at ease in their ignorance. What matters is not what God's Word means to you, but what God's Word means. God has spoken, and we should show we are taking him at his word by listening, heeding and responding.

Over and over again God has been pleased to richly bless me as I have pored over his Word in the course of my study of this subject, and nothing would make me happier than that this little book should be used by him to lead others into the joy and untainted happiness found in Christ, who declared himself to be the Lord of the Sabbath.

It has long been accepted that Christians may differ in their understanding and interpretation of some parts of the Bible, for example with regard to the 'last things', without this interfering with fellowship with those holding different views. These are secondary issues over which godly men and women have, often cautiously, reached different conclusions, and we respect them for it, whatever our own persuasion.

So, is the issue of the Sabbath in that same category of being 'secondary', or is it really primary? Even here, Christians differ. However, unlike some other differences of opinion regarding interpretation, this one impacts directly on the Christian's use of one day every week. Your view of the Sabbath is bound to affect how you conduct yourself on a Sunday. This being the case, we must accept that it is an issue of some importance and that there is some benefit to being clear in our own mind about it.

On the whole I have found that, for want of better terms, 'Sabbatarians' and 'Non-Sabbatarians' not only disagree with each other, but they tend to start from different points as they argue their positions. This does not help the dialogue between them!

Controversy concerning the Sabbath is of course not new. The title of this book quotes words spoken by Jesus to the Pharisees who objected to what he and his disciples were doing on the Sabbath (Matthew 12:1-8). Indeed, even from a cursory reading of the Gospels one can hardly miss the fact that the way Jesus used the Sabbath became a central and contentious issue. It has remained a contentious issue down the centuries since then, and, unhappily, it remains so today. If this book helps some who are troubled by the subject toward a clearer understanding, it will have served its purpose well, for a good understanding of God's Word is vital if we are to live lives pleasing to him (Colossians 1:9-10). Psalm 119 speaks repeatedly of the value of understanding (for example verses 34, 73, 104, 125, 144), while in the Proverbs Solomon is constantly urging it as of supreme importance (a few examples being 2:3-6,11; 3:13; 4:5-9; 16:16,22).

That said, it must be admitted there is no simple answer to this controversy. If there were, the matter would have been cleared up a long time ago. Much scholarly work has gone into producing books and articles from respected Christian leaders, some on one side, some on the other, of the debate. Whatever conclusions are reached in this book, the reader will be aware that they rest upon the writer's own theological position. This is precisely the reason why there is no simple answer. Where the Bible speaks clearly and unequivocally about something, man has an extraordinary capacity to find complications and ambiguities. That is his problem, not God's, and he will be held accountable for it at the last day.

Under a consideration of this subject a number of questions are bound to require addressing. Here are a few for you to think about. Are you able to give thoroughly biblical answers to these questions?

When did the Sabbath come into existence?

The Ten Commandments (including the fourth) were given to the Jewish nation, but were they intended to be limited to the Jews or are they wider, or even universal, in their application?

Are some aspects of the Ten Commandments prophetic and fulfilled in Christ in the sense of their being superseded and no longer relevant to, or binding upon, Christians?

Are we to see distinctions of application within the Ten Commandments, so that some are still applicable today while others are not (or less so)?

Are we to make a distinction between the Ten Commandments and any or all of the other laws given through Moses?

What is the relationship between law and grace?

What is the connection between the law of commandments and the law of love?

What is the relationship, if any, between 'the Sabbath' and 'the Lord's Day'?

How are we to decide what is legitimate for us as Christians to do on a Sunday? (Is even the question a valid one?)

Does the Christian church really have a biblical warrant for its practices on a Sunday and a mandate to preserve them, or is this something which has merely been 'borrowed' as a matter of convenience from an earlier and now obsolete tradition?

If you do regard the Fourth Commandment as still valid and finding its expression in 'the Lord's Day', how are you to conduct your affairs in a society which has moved away from virtually any recognition of keeping Sunday special? Is it right for the Christian church to seek to impose Sabbath principles upon society at large?

It should be clear that these and other related questions are by no means trivial, and yet they all have a bearing upon the main question before us in this book. This poses a dilemma, because to aim for an exhaustive analysis would not only take a great deal of time, it would run the serious risk of obscuring what I am setting out to do. Therefore, although many things will have to be left unsaid, it is hoped that nothing of importance will be glossed over and that enough will be said to enable the reader to 'fill in the gaps'.

How then should the task be approached? Having pondered the Word of God on this subject and earnestly sought its Author for understanding, I can only encourage the reader to do the same. Each chapter will therefore be presented somewhat in the form of a Bible study in which we endeavour to address and answer a number of questions which have a direct or indirect bearing on 'the Sabbath issue'. It is hoped that on the way the reader will, through study and meditation, come to a deeper appreciation of, and reverence for, God's Word, which will be beneficial in itself, and that by the end, when all the strands are woven together, a clearer picture will emerge concerning 'the Sabbath' and 'the Lord's Day', along with some of the practical implications.

This book is written from a clear conviction concerning the authority of Scripture. The Bible is God's Word, and as such should be sufficient for us in terms of defining what we should believe and practise. The deficiencies in our understanding may be remedied from this Book under the necessary enlightenment from the Holy Spirit and we should not actually need to look elsewhere. For some it may be very interesting to know what various people have contributed to the subject and what has been practised historically at different times down the centuries in the life of the Christian church. For others this same information might be disturbing or confusing. While not denying that there is a proper place for the help of men to aid us in our understanding of God's Word (why otherwise would books like this be written?), in a situation like this our ultimate conclusion must be based on what the Scriptures say, not on what men say about the Scriptures.

It is for this reason that quotations from others and examples from history are kept to a very minimum. One such quotation I will make now. In his little book, *Whatever Happened to the Ten Commandments?*, coming to the fourth, Ernest C Reisinger writes: 'Our generation is in desperate need of some biblical instruction concerning the Fourth Commandment.' After making some scathing comments about its treatment at the hands of various sections of the church, he adds: 'The Fourth Commandment is worthy of serious study because of its importance in our spiritual warfare and is critical for our corrupt generation.'[1]

It is from similar convictions that I have written this book. On the basis of these convictions I would urge the reader to examine prayerfully and carefully what he or she finds in these pages, to compare Scripture with Scripture, and to reach conclusions so firmly anchored in the bedrock of the Word of God that this book or any other help on the subject may thenceforth be rendered redundant. Any God-given human help serves its purpose only as it promotes and honours his Word.

A brief bibliography, together with some further notes, is included at the end for the sake of further study for those who wish to follow up the subject more fully.

A word of warning follows from what has just been said: this book is not intended to be an 'easy read'. It may not be particularly long, but it demands close and careful attention to the Bible. It will yield relatively little to those reluctant to invest their time in this way. However, equally, it is hoped that it will not be difficult to understand. God gave his Word to his people for their instruction and benefit, and by and large what we read in our Bibles is clear and straightforward in its meaning and we are to treat it as such, even though we admit we are not always as quick to understand as we might be. We should be suspicious of those who present us with teaching which seems to put a slant on the Bible, or any part of it, inconsistent with how it reads naturally to the spiritually-minded Christian desiring to honour and obey the Lord. No part of the Bible was intended to be accessible only to a select few. When he gave gifts of teaching to some men, God did so to help make the meaning of his Word *clear* to people (see Nehemiah 8:8,12 and Ephesians 4:11-13). My prayer is that those who read this book will be helped to a clearer understanding of what God's Word says on this important subject.

In the beginning

Agood place to begin is at the beginning! For our purposes the beginning is the creation account. Hardly have we embarked and set sail than for some there may be the very real danger of foundering on the reef of evolution. For those who do not accept the historicity of the Genesis account of creation, even though Jesus and his apostles clearly did (Luke 3:38; Matthew 19:4; Romans 5:12-21; 1 Corinthians 15:21-22,45-49; 1 Timothy 2:13-14; Jude 14), there is little point in continuing, for they shall never get into clear water.

To change the metaphor, without the foundation provided by Genesis the edifice being built is bound to collapse. If you as a reader have serious doubts in this area, then it is far better that you get to grips with the creation versus evolution controversy, because that really is a fundamental issue. There is now widely available much excellent, readable, scientifically sound literature which examines the foundations of 'popular evolution', exposing evolutionary hypotheses for what they are, and which confirms the veracity of the biblical account. Then you will be able to come back to the Word of God with renewed confidence. There are well-preserved and detailed specimens of atheistic evolution in books, but they won't be found in real life! There is nothing to fear from them. What is often presented as simple fact by the popular media is viewed very differently in serious scientific circles covering a wide range of disciplines.

What has creation got to do with the Sabbath?

Why go back to Genesis when the first mention of the Sabbath does not occur until the time of Moses (Exodus 16:23)? What has the creation account to do with the Sabbath? The answer is of course spelt out in Exodus 20:8-11—'Remember the Sabbath day, to keep it holy. Six days you shall labour and do all your work, but the seventh day is the Sabbath of the LORD your God. In it you shall do no work: you, nor your son, nor your daughter, nor your male servant, nor your female servant, nor your cattle, nor your stranger who is within your gates. *For in six days the LORD made the heavens and the earth, the sea, and all that is in them, and rested the seventh day.* Therefore the LORD blessed the Sabbath day and hallowed it.'

Let us start by making a number of important preliminary observations which are fairly self-evident in the commandment. In speaking to Israel, God instructed them (verse 8) to 'remember the Sabbath day, to keep it holy.' Then in verse 10 he explains: 'But the seventh day is the Sabbath of the Lord your God.' At this point therefore he is equating the seventh day with the Sabbath day. The word 'Sabbath' throughout the Old Testament is organically related to the word meaning 'cessation' or 'rest'. It means putting something to one side and leaving it alone, having nothing further to do with it for the time being. If we ask what this is, the context makes it quite clear, taking verses 9 and 10 together, that it is the work of the six previous days. Then, the cessation is comprehensive, indicating that everybody and everything associated with the Israelites, including servants and cattle and foreigners among them, were to be given rest, and, furthermore, that the responsibility for providing that rest lay with the Israelites themselves. We shall see in the course of this book that every one of these aspects is significant.

If we now ask why a rest of this kind should be required, God provides us with the answer in verse 11. He worked for six days and rested on the seventh, and, for some reason, he required the Israelites to do the same. For some reason? For what reason? It is vital that we ask what this reason is, because, as we will discover, it lies at the very heart of the matter. To say that they needed a break to recuperate after six days' work is not an adequate answer. It does not address the real issue. In fact it has very little, if anything, to do with the real issue. This is not to dispute the fact that people need regular periods of rest, nor that the seven day cycle has something to do with the constitution of men and women bound up with how God made them. That may be true, but the real issue before us here lies at the end of verse 11, where the Sabbath day is again identified with the seventh day, only this time not the last day of a seven-day cycle but the seventh day of creation.

Comparing what God says here through Moses with what he had said right at the beginning (Genesis 2:3) there is a difference in just one word. In Exodus the Lord says, referring to creation, that he blessed the *Sabbath*, whereas in Genesis he says he blessed the *seventh day*. In so saying, God is showing that his requirements in the Fourth Commandment are not arbitrary, to be followed without question or reason. God does not leave his people blindly to follow his rules. By this identification of the Sabbath with the seventh day of creation, he is investing the 'rest' of the seventh day with *meaning* for man, that man is to enter into, or participate in, his—God's—rest. It is a *Sabbath rest*. When in verse 11 we read, '*Therefore* the LORD blessed the Sabbath day and hallowed it', the reason hinges upon the significance of the seventh day of creation and the implication that there is a close connection between the two. A failure to recognize this will inevitably lead to doubt and confusion. It is remarkable how many books on this subject fail to probe the meaning of the rest on the seventh day of creation week or consider how it relates to the Sabbath of the Fourth Commandment or the Lord's Day of the New Testament.

That the Sabbath predates man's fall into sin is of fundamental importance and yet this too is so often overlooked when considering this subject. It concerns a practical aspect of man's relationship with his Maker which has nothing to do with his present sinfulness. In this respect, we might note in passing, it has a similar status to the marriage relationship which also predates the fall.

A couple of points need to be made here to prepare for what will be enlarged upon later. Firstly, although the Fourth Commandment focuses upon the Sabbath rest, we must not overlook that it actually sets out the pattern for work as well as the pattern for rest, basing both on creation. 'Six days you shall labour and do all your work ... For in six days the LORD made the heavens and the earth, the sea, and all that is in them.' 'But the seventh day is the Sabbath of the LORD your God ... [the LORD] rested the seventh day.'

Secondly, while there is clearly significance in the Sabbath being on the seventh day, the actual day is subservient to its purpose. That is, the blessing and the hallowing of the Sabbath day are connected with the rest and the purpose of the rest, and not with the number seven as such. The Sabbath memorial comes at the end of something completed. There is an 'all' in verse 9 and an 'all' in verse 11. For God, his work of creation was finished; for man, his work within the creation was to be finished for that week. The word 'all' in verse 9 seems to stress this. While obviously there would be work to do in the week which followed, for the week which was past the work was brought to a conclusion. The spirit of the Sabbath demanded that the work of the six previous days should have been viewed as completed rather than suspended. With this view, the Sabbath could be treated as a celebration with God of what had been accomplished and not an inconvenient interruption to an ongoing project.

Incidentally, with this identification of the weekly Sabbath with the seventh day of creation, *and also the identification of the six days of work with the six days of creation*, it is difficult to maintain, as some do, the notion that because there is no mention of 'evening and morning' after the seventh day of creation, the seventh day is a day without end, or the rest there intended for man was an eternal rest. We cannot argue from what is not said, only from what is said. If silence is significant, we have to prove it so. It seems to me that those who take this line are confusing things which differ.

It is eminently natural that there should be no reference to evening and morning at the end of the seventh day if we think why they are mentioned, for the evening and morning closed one stage of creation and opened another. Take a trivial example which those accustomed to supermarket shopping will appreciate. You are in a queue and finally reach the till. The person in front of you still has goods on the conveyor, so either you or she picks up the dividing bar provided for the purpose, which says something like 'Next customer' on it, placing it at right angles across the conveyor before you start to transfer your goods onto the belt, to make clear where her goods end and yours begin. When you have placed your last item there the next person behind you does the same as you did, placing the divider across the conveyor so that her goods don't get mixed up with yours. What happens if she is the last in the queue? No divider is placed after her goods. She has only one trolley full of goods just like everybody else and completes her checkout just like everybody else, but, being the last, there is no need for the divider.

The evening and morning divided the creation account into the days in which the separate stages took place. No divider was needed for the last of these. Nobody would query the fact that the seventh day of creation came to an end just like any other day.

It is true that creation was complete and that there was in that sense no more creative work to be done, but it is inconsistent semantically to take the 'day' of day seven to be any different from any of the other 'days', and Exodus 20:11 clearly indicates not only 24-hour days for creation, but also states this as a basis for a regular seven-day cycle. One cannot be categorical, but the language of Exodus 20 does seem to suggest that the seven-day cycle was established at the very beginning, even though there is no clear reference to it prior to this. There is, however, mention of seven days in Genesis 7:4; 8:10,12; while a 'week' is mentioned in Genesis 29:27. Joseph's official mourning for his father lasted seven days (Genesis 50:10). These occurrences in Genesis at least hint at the existence of a seven-day week. Then, further, in Exodus 7:25 there is mention of a passage of seven days after the Lord struck the waters of the Nile; and the eating of unleavened bread (Exodus 13:6) lasted seven days. The first mention of the Sabbath as such comes in Exodus 16 in connection with the provision of manna, where it is clearly tied in with the giving of the Law (in particular verses 4-5, 23, 27-30).

The Sabbath for a redeemed people

It is very unlikely that the seven day week was a new idea to the Israelites at this point in their history, any more than, say, that the offering of sacrifices was new, or that the laws engraved on the tablets of the Ten Commandments were previously unrecognized. Rather, these things are to be seen as a formalizing of what already existed, a clarification of principles which had been recognized down the centuries right from the beginning among God's people. In a sense, God was not telling the people anything new, but for the first time in history he was establishing the ground rules by clarifying, in writing, principles of conduct by which they were to continue in covenant relationship with him. God deemed that their new national identity should be undergirded by a written constitution, and this was it in the Ten Commandments and related laws. What had previously been understood in terms of right and wrong or what should or should not be done, revealed by God in various ways and sufficient for the relatively small number of his people as then existed, now required formal expression for the administration of their national life as the people of God. Here, perhaps for the first time, what he required of his people was brought into sharp focus. This would have been as true for the seven day week as for any of the other commandments. This is what God's Word does. As we read and gain understanding, enabled by the Holy Spirit, we are enlightened out of our ignorance, and our fuzzy ideas about what he is like and what he expects of us are resolved into well-defined forms so that we begin to see them clearly. It is with this end in view that this book has been written; so prayerfully and carefully examine what is written here in the light of God's Word; *read* this book, but *study* the Scriptures!

When Moses later reviewed the Ten Commandments in Deuteronomy 5, when the Israelites were just about to go into the land of promise, there was a difference in the way he referred to the Fourth Commandment (verses 12-15). Instead of creation, we find mention of deliverance from slavery. While there can be little doubt that it is the Exodus version which was inscribed on the stone tablets, Moses here added another dimension to the keeping of the Sabbath: 'And remember that you were a slave in the land of Egypt, and the LORD your God brought you out from there by a mighty hand and by an outstretched arm; therefore the LORD your God commanded you to keep the Sabbath day.' The Israelites were therefore to keep it in remembrance of what God had done in saving them out of the terrible tyranny of slavery in Egypt. In other words, there was a strong redemptive element involved in the keeping of the Sabbath. This needs to be examined further, but for now we may make the inference that while in slavery in Egypt the Israelites were almost certainly denied the privilege of taking time out for the worship of God—see in particular Exodus 3:18; 5:1-3,8; 7:16; 8:1,8,20, etc. Sabbath observance therefore had the worship of God in view, with redemption as well as creation in mind. In addition, it was to set the pattern for how they were to treat any who were soon to be in servitude to them, whether servants or foreigners.

Two key words for understanding the Sabbath

Having established the fact the Sabbath day of the Ten Commandments is identified with the seventh day of creation, we are now in a position to examine what God says of it. In Genesis (2:3) he says essentially two fundamental things: he *blessed* it, and he *sanctified* it. This is repeated in Exodus 20:11, while in verse 10 there is the additional subservient information that it is, for Israel at least, 'the Sabbath of *the LORD your God*,' which embraces two further points: firstly that it is of (or 'to', NIV) *the LORD*, and secondly that it is of the LORD *your* God. Both aspects are significant. When I say that the additional information is for Israel *at least*, there may be some question about to whom this subservient statement applies. But from the primary declaration, that God blessed and sanctified the Sabbath, because it was made at the time of the creation, and made to a perfect, unfallen creation at that, we must draw the conclusion that it was originally intended for the whole of mankind. Why this should be the case, and how man's fall into sin has affected it, will be addressed later in this book.

For the remainder of this chapter, though, the two primary points will be taken in turn.

(a) The day which is blessed

First of all, what does it mean that God *blessed* the seventh day? What is to be understood by the term? To put it as simply as possible, God's blessing imparts happiness in the truest, fullest, most meaningful sense of the word. When we understand what it means, we realize that we can have no real happiness apart from him, while in him we can be nothing but happy. There is a lovely statement in Proverbs 10:22, which says: 'The blessing of the LORD makes rich, and he adds no sorrow with it.' The nature of the poetry forbids us to restrict this to a pecuniary sense or to view it from a mercenary perspective, for the blessing is contrasted with *sorrow*, and we are intended to recognize the fullness of the one in the absence of the other. So many earthly joys are tinged with sorrow; not so the blessing of the Lord. Of so much earthly happiness, we enjoy it while we can because we know it will not last; not so with the blessing of the Lord. The blessing of the Lord is associated with true riches, the 'solid joys and lasting treasure' which, as John Newton said, 'none but Zion's children know.'

A study of the way the Bible uses the word 'blessed' is a vastly rewarding exercise but lies outside the scope of this book. The Bible speaks of 'blessing' in a number of ways. Often we read of God blessing his people; sometimes we read of men blessing others. When God blesses his people it involves his giving and their receiving (ponder, for example, the scope of his blessing described in Ephesians 1:3-14). When one man blesses another, it is usually a declaration of that person being blessed by God, or tantamount to a prayer for the same, or even prophetic (for example, Genesis 14:19; 24:60; 28:1; 48:20; Numbers 6:22-27; 22:6; Matthew 5:44).

Here, however, it is not a *person* being blessed but a *day*. How can something inanimate and as intangible as a period of time be blessed? What does it mean? Deuteronomy 28:4-5 helps fill out the picture for us. God is speaking of the blessings he promises his people when they are diligently obedient to him: blessings which shall 'come upon' them and 'overtake' them, or 'accompany' them (verse 2). This is a lovely expression of the way his generous beneficence bears down upon his people rather like a flood, overwhelming them with its abundant power and carrying them along in its current. Among the blessings we read (verses 4-5): 'Blessed shall be the fruit of your body, the produce of your ground and the increase of your herds, the increase of your cattle and the offspring of your flocks. Blessed shall be your basket and your kneading bowl.' Instead of children being born to die of disease, or crops being blighted, or herds struggling to survive on parched and unproductive soil, instead of the people having to scrimp and save, or to scratch an existence in inhospitable surroundings, they will find health and prosperity, plenty and security and satisfaction. Their basket will be full, as will their kneading bowl, without their having to cast about for supplements. Clearly the meaning is that these things will be blessed to God's people, and that in them they will recognize his rich provision.

Similarly, when God blessed the seventh day, we are to understand the day to be blessed in the same way as the basket was blessed, or the kneading bowl was blessed. As with these, the day was blessed to those to whom it was provided. In the beginning, when God blessed the seventh day, it was blessed to Adam and Eve. Here we return to what has just been said, that when God blesses his people, he gives and they receive. We cannot understand what it means that God blessed the seventh day without asking *for whom* it was blessed. Until we have thought about this the statement remains meaningless. God made the day to be a blessing *to man*. When God blessed the seventh day it was with the specific intention that man should be the recipient. What is remarkable is that this blessing was pronounced into a whole and perfect creation, in which Adam and Eve were perfectly happy and, we might think, fully blessed, notwithstanding the fact that they were for a time on a kind of probation in the garden.

Why then should God pronounce a blessing upon the seventh day for Adam and Eve to enter into, or was he simply declaring that, his creation now being complete and 'very good', from now on man was to enter into the benefit of it? Those who argue this way are totally dependent upon it being significant that there is no stated demarcation of the end of the seventh day. Or is this the inauguration of the seven day week, on which the seventh day was to be of special significance, of special 'blessing', to unfallen man? For the moment these important questions will be left hanging, to be pondered until we return to them later on.

(b) The day which is sanctified

God not only blessed the seventh day, he also 'sanctified' it. This brings us to the second important aspect of the seventh day, and again we look into the meaning of the word. When a person or an object is said to be sanctified it means it is set apart for a special purpose. So, for example, Aaron and his sons were sanctified (or consecrated) to the service of the priesthood (Exodus 28:41). Likewise the meat and bread of Exodus 29:33-34 were said to be sanctified, or made holy, because they were provided for a very special purpose by the Lord in the course of Aaron's ordination. The altar, too, was sanctified for its unique and holy use (Exodus 29:37). Jesus, praying for his disciples, as he declares that they no more belong to the world than he does, asks his Father, 'Sanctify them by Your truth. Your word is truth' (John 17:16-17). The Christian belongs to Christ, not to the world; the Christian is therefore to 'sanctify the Lord God' in his heart (1 Peter 3:15). The place of exclusive right in the heart of the Christian is given to Christ the Lord. If you are a Christian reading this, have you fully acknowledged this truth? When Jesus confirmed the lawyer's reading of the law: 'You shall love the LORD your God with all your heart, with all your soul, with all your strength, and with all your mind' (Luke 10:27) we cannot mistake that the 'all' is comprehensive, and that in its fourfold application it leaves no area of our being excluded from total devotion to God. This is what sanctification is all about. Or, to use an equivalent word, this is what holiness is all about. We are separated from the world in our heart, soul, strength and mind that we might be completely dedicated to God in heart, soul, strength and mind.

So when God sanctified the seventh day, he made it holy, investing exclusive rights in it, declaring it to be *his* day in a sense which, observe, he did not apply to any other day. This could not of course imply that every other day was not his day, or that he had limited rights in any other day. Therefore we are bound logically to draw the conclusion that there was something special about the seventh day that he should so distinguish it. As time is also part of the created order, belonging essentially to the creation and therefore to man within the creation, making man a creature of time, inevitably man must therefore come to the seventh day, and thereupon enter what God has designated his own day. The implication of this is inescapable, namely that man must fit into the pattern which God has imprinted upon the day. If it is God's holy day—and it is, because God has said so—then man who makes an appearance on God's holy day must himself be holy. For on God's holy day everything in all creation needs must, by definition, conform to the holiness which characterizes what God has set apart for himself.

In exactly the same way as we cannot understand what it means to bless the seventh day without asking to whom it is blessed, neither can we understand what it means to sanctify the day without asking to whom it is sanctified. On the one hand the day is blessed to man; on the other it is sanctified to God. That is, God set aside the day for himself. The same kind of question arises: Why did he do this? Was it simply on account of his having finished his work, so that now he could, as we might say of our own completed work, 'sit back and enjoy it'? Again, is this why there is no stated demarcation of the end of the seventh day?

The day which is both blessed and sanctified
God did not just bless the seventh day, he sanctified it; he did not just sanctify it, he blessed it. As we now draw these two aspects together, like the

merging of the two images of binocular vision, we see the coming together of man and God. It is God's day, because he made it, and it is special to him because he sanctified it. At the same time it is made for man, because God blessed it, and it is this day which is to provide the time channel through which God's blessing is to be poured out upon man (or 'into man' might better convey the meaning). Our focus sees not God with one eye and man with the other, but man in the presence of God, man receiving from God, man learning from his God and growing in the knowledge of the One by whom he is fully known, and so man worshipping and enjoying God his Maker with ever-increasing understanding and fullness.

Have you ever asked God's blessing upon your life, or for him to bless you with some particular provision? Have you ever thought, as you have asked, or as you have yearned, or as you have pleaded, that if you are asking aright you are really asking through it to be brought into greater intimacy with him? What you seek to wrest from his hand is no blessing; what you want because you want it without regard for whether he wants it for you is no blessing either. We read of the Israelites in the desert that at one point God gave them things they lusted after (no mincing of words there!), but sent leanness into their souls (Psalm 106:13-15). They had so put God's works out of their minds that it is said they had forgotten them. They did not seek his counsel. All they wanted was to satisfy their own selfish and sinful cravings. To receive the gift without the giver is not blessing, but judgement.

If we are to understand the significance of the Sabbath, then, we must see these two things as going hand in hand. The one is that God blessed it *to man,* that is, it was made for man, for his benefit, for his happiness, for his proper fulfilment in life; the other is that God sanctified it, that is, he set it apart *for himself.* Which means that man's blessing from the Sabbath can be derived only in relationship with God, not independently of him.

Before we even begin to address the question as to whether we are dealing with a seven day cycle or the inauguration of a day without a terminus, let us hold firmly in our grasp the unmistakable dual aspect of the 'day' we have just been considering, for this really is the key to everything which follows. Whatever our view of the Sabbath, it must see man in the presence of God, and it must involve man in fellowship with God. That is its essence. Every consideration which is not subservient to this is therefore irrelevant.

Whose Sabbath is it?

Thus far we have been examining the common ground on this subject between Exodus 20 and Genesis 2, and have spent some time thinking about what is absolutely fundamental. Moving on now, let us pick up on what was observed earlier, that Exodus 20:10 informs us, concerning Israel at least, that 'the seventh day is the Sabbath of the LORD your God,' which contains two further ingredients: firstly that it is the Sabbath of *the LORD*, and secondly that it is the Sabbath of the LORD *your God*.

Because the Bible is a history of revelation we should expect fuller information the further we progress through its pages. There is a gradual development of what God reveals of himself and his purposes as history unfolds. A child who grows into manhood or womanhood, of necessity builds upon earlier knowledge and experience. This earlier knowledge and experience contribute to an understanding and appreciation of more recent experience, and their combined effect is often to reassess the old more accurately in the light of it. We can sometimes look back on happenings earlier in our lives and smile inwardly at our former naivety in the way we then viewed them. Nevertheless, without those experiences we would never have reached our present state of maturity to be in a position so to view them. They were an essential part of our development. We see things in them now that we never dreamt of or only dimly perceived at the time.

Now God's Word comes to us with full authority right from the beginning in Genesis 1, spoken by One who knows the end from the beginning. If we had followed through from the beginning without any further knowledge we might have learned certain things from what was being revealed and wondered where it was all leading. Later on we might exclaim, 'Now I understand what he meant when he said....' That is not to imply any deficiency in what God had said, only that our understanding of its full significance was waiting upon the arrival of fuller revelation, at which point we become able to interpret it more completely. The strategy in this book largely follows these lines, going back to the beginning and gradually building up the picture from scratch. You too may wonder where it is all leading, but it is an essential part of the process which should lead to the ultimate, 'Now I understand....'

However, something more than what we might call a natural development of revelation is required to account for the differences between what is stated in Genesis 2 and what we read in Exodus 20. It is not just that God is saying something further now which he could, had he wished, have said in the first place. In fact, every development in revelation from God to man has its rationale in the events of history, being spoken into the prevailing circumstances at the appropriate moment. So what in particular accounts for the difference between Genesis 2 and Exodus 20? Just this: the former was applicable to sinless man in a perfect creation; the latter was addressed to fallen man in a creation under a curse on account of his disobedience. Hence, as we shall see, there is need for these two further explanatory statements.

From what has been said so far, the devastating effects of the fall upon the Sabbath will be obvious. The entry of sin into the world with all its horrible consequences severed at a stroke what was to have been the noblest and highest activity of man: his fellowship with God. He could still work, but the meaning of work was now destroyed because it could no longer be done in its proper context. The Sabbath rest now became an empty void, because fellowship with God had been destroyed. This was a tragedy of the first order. It is perhaps no coincidence that the 'rest' of the Sabbath finds no specific mention in the Word of God until we reach Exodus 16 and 20 and the Ten Commandments (although the preservation of the seven day cycle clearly had persisted, as indeed it has down to our own day), and even there the Sabbath has to be introduced as a piece of legislation.

The Sabbath of *the LORD* indicates emphatically that it is *his* day. Because of the entry of sin into the world it has become necessary to spell out the fact to people that it is not their day for them to do as they will, but his day in which they are to do as he wills. This is saying much the same thing as that the Lord sanctified the day, but it is saying it in more specific language because it is addressing people who have lost that clear perspective. Furthermore, in saying it is the Sabbath of the LORD *your God*, attention is now being drawn to the fact that there is a relationship between the people and the Lord which does not necessarily apply to mankind in general. There are many for whom the LORD is not their God, but those who do find themselves under his lordship are reminded that their Lord has designated this day both for their benefit and for his own honour.

We observe in this language what appears to be a narrowing down of application. Once, at the beginning, the seventh day was blessed to man without qualification. Now, however, it is blessed to those brought into covenant relationship with God; and while these commandments formed the *terms* of the covenant, the relationship itself was established by God's gracious intervention in liberating the people from bondage (Exodus 20:2). Though the words are so targeted, it cannot be deduced that the intended scope of the Sabbath has changed, for nothing can be permitted to diminish the lustre of what God created perfect, including his declaration about the purpose of the seventh day. Man's abuse of the creation, and even the curse God has himself imposed on it on man's account, do not annul what God originally intended, and his purposes are on track for the deliverance of the creation itself from bondage to corruption. See Romans 8:20-23 and Colossians 2:19 in context.

The nature of the function designated by God for the seventh day requires that it be viewed in its organic connection with his creative work of the six preceding days. When Jesus asserted that the Sabbath was made for man (Mark 2:27) he was answering a point of law about the Fourth Commandment. His answer, though, is not that the Sabbath *law* was made for man, but that the Sabbath *itself* was made for man, so that he is tracing back through the law to the foundation upon which the law is based, namely the seventh day of creation. God had created the whole of the universe in six days (Exodus 20:11); nothing was created on the seventh day, because the whole of creation was complete. God did not make anything *on* the seventh day: rather, he made the seventh day itself to be the Sabbath—for man. It was made not for some men, not for a chosen few, but for man universally. We will return to this in due course. For the present, though, we conclude that what God intends for, and therefore requires of, all people, is placed into the hands of his chosen people that they, by his grace, might be given the understanding to live as he intended. This is what was said earlier, that the responsibility for the maintenance of the Sabbath rest was entrusted to God's people. Thus the Fourth Commandment, equally with the other nine, is part of the expression of what God intends for man if he is to enjoy his relationship with him in perfection.

A sign

When Moses went up to the top of the mountain of Sinai to receive the law for his people, he remained there for forty days (Deuteronomy 9:9-11). However, the Ten Commandments which were inscribed by the Lord himself on two tablets of stone, described in Deuteronomy 9:9 as 'the tablets of the covenant', and given to Moses at the end of that period, had already been spoken in the hearing of the people before Moses made that ascent (Exodus 19:25; 20:19-21; Deuteronomy 5:22-24). Whatever followed in the way of other laws given on Sinai, these all rested upon the basis of the covenant already established and had no meaning apart from it. The Ten Commandments were unique and foundational, written by the finger of God and later housed in the ark of the covenant in the place on earth representing his presence, accessible only through the blood of sacrifice. If anyone were to ask what was required of him or her as one of God's covenant people, there was the ultimate reference, for there, and nowhere else, were the terms of the covenant.

However, the word 'covenant' appears again in connection with the Sabbath in Exodus 31:12-18 (see verse 16, but please read the whole section as reference will later be made more extensively to it). Significantly, this comes at the conclusion of the time Moses spent at the top of Sinai, forming as it were the Lord's parting words to his servant as he gives into his charge the two tablets of stone containing the Ten Commandments. This passage makes sombre reading with its repeated mention of the death penalty for desecration of the Sabbath and being 'cut off' from the people. It is undoubtedly on account of these instructions that the penalty was imposed upon the Sabbath breaker in Numbers 15:32-36 (of which more later).

Was the Sabbath a covenant for the Jews?

It has been suggested by some that because this passage (Exodus 31:12-18) describes the Sabbath in terms of a covenant for the Israelite nation (verses 16-17) and comes at the conclusion of detailed instructions about ceremonies which were clearly specific to the Jews (Exodus 25 to 31), it is therefore inappropriate to seek to impose its regulations upon anyone else. It is further argued that this proves the Fourth Commandment to be specific to Israel and not binding upon the New Testament church. However, this argument could be applied to the Ten Commandments themselves, for the introduction in Exodus 20:2 unequivocally applies them to those brought out of slavery in Egypt. This line of reasoning is fundamentally flawed, as will become apparent.

In reality this passage provides one of the strongest arguments why the Sabbath *is* binding upon the New Testament church. The Ten Commandments, and in particular the fourth, were given under the umbrella of redemption. The Israelites had been redeemed from physical slavery in Egypt, which indeed also had a strong spiritual element to it, that they might belong to God. As such they were brought under his covenant which was intended for their eternal good. The Sabbath emphasised their unique relationship with God. It was something which no other nation knew anything about, and as such was a sign, a witness, to all that they were God's people.

As we look at the origin of the Sabbath and its purpose (which we have begun to do), and as later we will look at its restoration, we will discover that it has relevance uniquely and supremely to us and that it is a tragedy that there are *Christians* who would make light of it. The Sabbath was *not* a covenant as such (and it cannot be so argued from this passage) but a creation ordinance. Verse 16 speaks of the Sabbath being *observed* as a perpetual covenant, but verse 17 says that it *is* a sign. (There is no verb in the original, and although the NIV translates it as 'It will be a sign', presumably this is only because at the time of it being spoken the formal observance was considered to be in the future, Moses not yet having come down from the mountain.) What this means is that observance of the Sabbath by Israel functioned as a sign that they were in covenant relationship with God. This is not so different from what is described as the covenant of circumcision in Genesis 17, where, in verse 10, the covenant is stated to be circumcision, whereas in verse 11 circumcision is said to be a *sign* of the covenant between God and Abraham. What emerges from these parallel cases is that the covenant itself is the agreement between God and Israel, or between God and Abraham and his descendants (as the case may be), that they will be his people, distinct from all others, to belong exclusively to him, and that their conduct in the world would *signify* this to others.

So the Sabbath was not the covenant as such, nor was it the *foundation* of the covenant relationship between God and his people. What Exodus 31:12-17 is describing is the *fundamental outworking* of that covenant. Anticipating what will be said later, Sabbath observance, rightly understood, remains a powerful witness in our own day. It tells people that we belong to the Lord, and that this day is for our appointed meeting with him. It declares to them that we love him, and that he is first in our thinking and in our lives. It is our badge of distinctiveness, testifying not to what we have achieved but to what God has made us and called us to be. In other words, it is a sign of a covenant relationship between the Lord and his people.

So let us ask the question again: If the Sabbath was given as a sign between the Lord and the Israelites (Exodus 31:13,17), and if it was given 'as a perpetual covenant' (Exodus 31:16), does this not mean that the Sabbath was instituted specifically for Israel and has no relevance to any other nation or individual?

It is true that the Sabbath had a very special place in the relationship between the Israelites and their God which seemed to go beyond what was stated in the Ten Commandments, and there was indeed a covenantal aspect to it relating to their national life (compare 2 Chronicles 36:21; Leviticus 26:34-43). However, it wasn't the Fourth Commandment *as such* which was the covenant, and therefore those who say the commandment related only to covenant Israel and so either no longer applies to us or is not relevant to us have come to a wrong conclusion. What Exodus 31:16 is saying of the Israelites is that they were very specifically to place themselves under oath unfailingly to observe the Sabbath because of its supreme importance in connection with their relationship to God. What God did for national Israel was to take the Fourth Commandment and use it as a sort of defining basis for the covenant between them. There is a very good reason for this as will emerge in due course if it is not already apparent. However, the Sabbath remains what it was, a creation ordinance, and if God chose to use it for a specific purpose for national Israel, this does not in any way affect how the Fourth Commandment relates to us. There was no exclusiveness about it for the Israelite nation.

More will be said of this shortly, but for the moment we summarize by saying that the Ten Commandments formed the terms of the covenant between God and his people, and he singled out the fourth of these, attaching to it a special significance on account, firstly, of what it represented, and, secondly, what it publicly signified.

However, all this has raised an important question which will need to be addressed sooner or later, which is: To whom *do* the Ten Commandments apply? If they, not to mention all the other laws given through Moses, were given specifically to the Jews, and if they formed the constitutional document for the Jewish nation, then to what extent are they to be applied more widely—either to society in general or to the Christian church in particular? I shall attempt to deal with this in the next chapter insofar as it relates to the subject before us, though an extended treatment is beyond the scope of this book.

Who are God's people?

It may seem surprising to be asked what the phrase 'God's people' means. However, it tends to be used by Christians in a rather loose and undefined manner, often applying the term more or less equally to the Old Testament nation of Israel and the Christian church without distinction, and therefore making application without distinction, whereas the Bible makes very clear distinctions (for example, Hosea 1:10; Romans 9:6). In one sense it is true that it was to the nation of Israel that God gave his law, but it should be borne in mind that their national identity as the people of God did not actually come into being in a formal sense until the giving of the law, for the law formed the constitution upon which this identity was established. What I am saying is that it might be more helpful to think in terms of the nation belonging to the law rather than the law belonging to the nation. In the latter case, if it had simply been *their* law, the law would have become obsolete had the nation come to an end. Indeed, the future of the nation appeared to be very much in question on more than one occasion.

All flesh is as grass, but it is the word of the LORD which endures for ever (1 Peter 1:24-25), and the security of nations depends upon his word, as was demonstrated over and over again in Israel's history. The law of God did not fluctuate in its authority, it did not have its ups and downs in its relevance, it did not alter in its meaning. The nation of Israel on the other hand went through all manner of vicissitudes, and their condition at any one time was directly related to their reverence for God's law. God does not tie his word to things which change that it might change with them.

So, God did not give the law to the nation for it to be moulded by them. Rather, he wedded the nation to his law for them to be guided by it. It can arguably be said that he created the nation in the giving of the law to the descendants of Israel. Having made a covenant with Abraham to be God to him and his descendants after him (Genesis 17:7-8) he now gave them a national identity and a land in which to live. The law identified Israel not as a people group *among* other people groups but as a people group *different from* other people groups. The law was established upon a vertical relationship with God rather than a horizontal relationship with men. So when we read, for example, about the 'sign between Me and the children of Israel' (Exodus 31:17) it is important that we think of 'the children of Israel', or, 'the Israelites', less in genetic or geographic terms and more in spiritual terms, because this has to do in the first place with a relationship with God and not with their national identity in a secular sense. It pointed to their being singled out by God to be holy to him (verse 13).

Covenant or sign—what's the difference?

Returning to the claim that the Sabbath was a covenant made exclusively with the Jews and therefore applied solely to them, and that it was as such incorporated into the Ten Commandments, a careful exposition of Exodus 31:12-18 actually casts it in a very different light. The word which is foremost in this passage is not 'covenant', but 'sign', and although there is undoubtedly a covenantal *aspect* to the Sabbath, this passage puts it very firmly in the context of a sign: the Sabbath would serve as a sign of that covenant (verses 16-17), *signifying* that those observing it were God's special people, consecrated to him and brought into a unique relationship with him (verse 13). We need first and foremost from this passage to understand what this sign signifies, and when that is clear we will appreciate the mention of its covenantal significance.

I have run the risk of some repetition (though I have come at it from different angles) in order to make a point and prepare the way forward. What we now need to do is to examine this passage in Exodus 31 in greater detail.

For the remainder of this chapter we will focus upon the meaning of this sign. We have observed that it makes sombre reading with the repeated mention of the death penalty for failure to observe the Sabbath. The first thing to note therefore is its *importance*. This is made clear from the outset: 'Surely My Sabbaths you shall keep' (verse 13). This is something which *must* be done. It is an imperative, not an option. It is top of the list, not somewhere half way down or at the lower end of their priorities. So why?

'It is a sign between Me and you' (verse 13); 'It is a sign between Me and the children of Israel' (verse 17). The implication is clear, that there is some special tie between God and his people. To take an illustration, it is common practice for a couple to exchange rings on their wedding day. The rings in themselves are of relatively little value, even though they may be made of a precious metal. Furthermore, the rings in themselves are not functional—they merely sit on the fourth finger of the hand and serve no outwardly useful purpose. But when, say, the husband observes the ring he has given his wife on her finger, it reminds him that she belongs to him, and when he observes the ring on his own finger it reminds him that he belongs to her. There is an exclusive bond between them: they have covenanted together as man and wife, and the rings serve as a sign of the fact. It is a sign to them, and it is also by implication a sign to others. Why would a woman deliberately leave her ring off when she goes out into society? Whatever answer you come up with can only be detrimental to their marriage relationship. In a good marriage it could be said that the rings are worn as a perpetual covenant 'till death do us part'. The rings themselves of course are not the covenant, but their presence and significance are inseparable from the covenant which has been made between 'this man and this woman'.

Unlike the rings in this illustration, the Sabbath was intended to be of more than 'relatively little value'. When the Sabbath was observed in the way God intended, it was a sign of a special, even an exclusive, relationship between him and his people. It was, for the Israelites, a regular, visible, practical, functional, reminder of what it meant to be in covenant relationship with God. Why would an Israelite deliberately leave off observance of the Sabbath? Again, whatever answer you come up with can only be detrimental to what it signified of the relationship between that person and his or her God.

Why the death penalty? Isn't that a bit severe, to put it mildly? We will return to this in a moment. First let us look a bit more closely at the sign and consider what comes out of its observance. In verse 13 Sabbath observance is described as a sign between God and his people that they may *know* that he is the Lord who sanctifies them. Keeping the Sabbath was therefore to be instructive, reminding the people that they were set apart by God and to God. He had called them, he had delivered them, he had blessed them, and he had done all these things to make them exclusively his—his special possession. By keeping the Sabbath they would 'know' it. This means a great deal more than the kind of knowledge acquired when someone studies for an examination. By doing what God had commanded they would enter into an understanding of what it all meant; that is, they would enter into the experience of what the covenant meant. Returning to the illustration of the wedding rings, the exchange of the rings is a sign of the covenant the couple have made, but they can only enter into the experience of the meaning of their covenant as they live together as man and wife. The rings *betoken* their privileges, rights and responsibilities toward one another, but they must then enter into the reality of what marriage is all about by *using* their privileges and rights and *fulfilling* their responsibilities toward each other. It is only when they do so that they can truly *know* what marriage is.

Similarly, having the Sabbath as a sign was one thing, but its observance enabled the Israelite to get a taste of the reality of his or her relationship with God. This is why God had given it. The day was intended to be very special to the people, for God said, 'it is holy to you' (verse 14). They were to guard it as very precious and use it accordingly. How were they to guard it? Certainly by avoiding working on that day. How were they to use it? Certainly by anything and everything which would promote intimacy of fellowship with their redeemer God.

Not only was the day holy to the Israelites, it was also 'holy to the Lord' (verse 15). God is saying here that it had special significance to him. But, as we see every time we consider the Sabbath, in whatever context, God and his people are there seen together. On the one hand the day was 'holy to the people' so that they could satisfy their need of fellowship with God; on the other, it was 'holy to the Lord' so that he could fulfil his desire for fellowship with his people. We say it with reverence and awe, that God went to such lengths to redeem his people from slavery in Egypt not that he might subsequently cast them off or ignore them, but in order to take pleasure in them and provide for them and show them the fullness of his love for them. The linking with creation again in verse 17 reminds us of the satisfaction of God with his completed, perfect creation, and that his enjoyment of it was very much bound up with the pinnacle of that creation, namely the creation of man, made in his image, capable of, and intended for, fellowship with him.

Sadly, though, sin entered the world, and consequently this fellowship was breached. What we see here is, as yet in shadowy form, the remedy supplied by God for the closing of the breach. These words are spoken into a sinful world, and to a sinful nation. Were it not for sin, the imperative of the command would not be necessary, and this special provision would be superfluous.

On pain of death

Now we must come to the matter of being 'cut off' (verse 14) and being 'put to death' (verses 14, 15). In the light of the New Testament we can see it was vital to preserve the truth down the generations until the coming of Christ into the world (Romans 9:4, etc.), which might account for such severity against disobedience in this area. But, more than that, we can see that lack of regard for the observance of the Sabbath implied lack of regard for the covenant between God and his people, and effectively struck the note of defiance that man was going to go his own way. 'There is a way that seems right to a man, but its end is the way of death' (Proverbs 14:12; 16:25). Neglect of Sabbath observance struck at the very heart of the relationship between God and man. It rendered it void. There could be only one ultimate consequence for this: the separation of which it spoke for time would result in separation for eternity. Whichever way we look at it, the consequence was death. To scorn the Sabbath was to scorn its Lord, and to scorn its Lord meant to scorn redemption (compare Hebrews 10:26-31). To scorn redemption was to place man beyond hope, left to face only wrath and eternal punishment. The death penalty declared by God himself was a very serious reminder of what desecration of the Sabbath was really all about.

We can now turn to Numbers 15:32-36 and the account of the death penalty imposed upon a Sabbath-breaker. At first sight it looks, to say the least, an 'over-the-top' reaction. 'After all, the poor man was only gathering sticks', we might say, and we might be exceedingly disturbed by what was decided in his case. Indeed, those who found him, though they knew he was breaking the Sabbath command and that this was a serious matter, were unsure as to what should be done with him. The response, we note, came not from man, not from Moses, but from the Lord, and it was unequivocal: the man must die. 'But why?' we still ask. This is where we are reminded of the importance of considering the context. In this chapter of the book of Numbers we read of laws concerning two categories of disobedience: unintentional (verses 22-29) and presumptuous (verses 30-31); and of the importance of giving careful heed to God's law (verses 37-41). The case of the Sabbath-breaker is placed here as an example of the second category of disobedience. Far from being a 'poor man only gathering sticks' he was in fact flagrantly flouting what he knew to be a clear command of God. This judgement is almost certainly recorded here as an illustration of 'despising the word of the LORD' mentioned in the previous two verses.

That is why the people who came across him did not merely reprove him or report him, but took him into custody. His action was a demonstration that he despised God's word and that if he wanted to go out and do work he was going to do it no matter what anybody said. This man, acting in defiance of Moses and the laws given through him, was actually acting in defiance of God. He who had despised the need for, and the way of, forgiveness, found himself summarily ushered into the consequence of departing this life without God. He was of that class of people whose attitude is that they will live as they please and 'take what's coming to them' without any favours, little realizing the significance of those awful words: 'His guilt shall be upon him.'

If the Sabbath was a sign between God and his people, it was also by implication a sign in a different sense to those outside the relationship. It could not be otherwise, because its observance was so public and different from how other people conducted their affairs. Because it was a sign for all to see, it served for the instruction of those as yet outside the covenant. Many have thought of the Sabbath in terms of what is permitted or not permitted by way of activity (work) on the day. I am not allowed to work on this day, so how do I use my time? However, if the Sabbath was being kept in the way God intended it should, others would not have seen the Israelites sitting around with their feet up, or spending their time in masterly inactivity, whiling away the interminable hours until they could get back to their daily routine. Leviticus 23:3 describes the Sabbath as being a day for 'a holy convocation' or 'sacred assembly'. It was a day for the people to gather together. For what purpose? Although the Scripture does not say so directly at this point, enough has been ascertained for us to understand that it was intended as a day for worshipping the Lord.

Some have argued that 'worship' and 'service' mean the same thing, and that we worship God as we serve him, and we serve him as we worship him. A careful examination of the biblical words and their use indicates clear distinctions which put the lid on the activistic notions of those who always want to be 'up and doing' as if this were the be-all and end-all of worship. The Sabbath gave the people of God the opportunity to gather together for the explicit purpose of praising him and spending time in his presence to learn from him, to make something in practice of the relationship they had with him in theory. It was given so that they might enjoy and be enriched in their relationship with God. This really was the sign to outsiders. These people lived differently. They didn't do this, and they didn't do that: they seemed to have a rigorous standard of righteousness which cut across the grain of what most people's concept of the 'good life' represented. So what did they do? If for six days of the week people saw what they didn't do, on the Sabbath they saw what they did do! They delighted in God, and met together to worship him. This, and perhaps this alone definitively, marked them out as different. Others might be morally upright (at least outwardly), others might be God fearing and be bound by rules and regulations which reflected that. But the Sabbath was something different! It represented a powerful witness to what lies at the heart of vital religion: a living relationship with the living God.

The place of the law

W e cannot really consider the question of the Sabbath without reference to its place in the Ten Commandments, and it is necessary for this reason to consider the commandments as a whole, which we will now do.[2] A number of passages in the New Testament have been used to undermine the authority of the law, and if the Ten Commandments are thereby weakened, so in particular is the fourth of them. Some of these passages must therefore be more closely scrutinized to see what they are really saying.

Often quoted when the law is mentioned is Romans 6:14 where Paul says we are not under law but under grace, and it is invariably prefaced with the word, 'But…'. In some Christian circles there appears to be a fear of making too much of the law of God lest the charge be laid against them that they are becoming legalistic; and perhaps some, after reading the preceding chapters, may nevertheless still have a niggling suspicion at the back of their minds that this is the direction in which this book is heading!

There does seem to be widespread ignorance among Christians these days about the place and relevance of the law. What did Jesus mean when he said that he came to *fulfil* the law, and that not one jot or tittle would pass from the law until all was fulfilled (Matthew 5:17,18)? Was he referring to the entire law of Moses, or only part of it or certain aspects of it? And when was all 'fulfilled' (if indeed it has been fulfilled)? And if it has been fulfilled does this mean that the law is a thing of the past? The verses which follow (Matthew 5:19-20) make one thing clear: whatever the commandments were that he was referring to, they remain in force in the kingdom of heaven, that is, in the time of the New Testament church. The question is: Exactly what are 'these commandments'?

Several questions have just been asked which need to be answered. Commencing with some comments about the place of the law in general, the first thing to be said is that there is not really so much mystery about this matter as some make out. It is helpful to recognize that the law God gave to Moses falls into about three fairly well defined categories.[3] First of all there are the Ten Commandments which stand as an entity of their own and relate essentially to the moral life of the people, encompassing in a single sweep every aspect of their personal and corporate life. Then there are many laws governing the social and political life of the Israelites (including health and welfare). And finally there are laws which relate to what might be described as their religious life—ceremonies to be performed in connection with their worship of God and his service. This is not to deny that there may be some overlap in these latter two to make it unclear where one category ends and another begins. This is to be expected because the requirements of ceremonial aspects of the law pervaded the whole of their lives.

Because this book is concerned with the Fourth Commandment, we ought to stop to examine what has just been said about the uniqueness and distinctness of the Ten Commandments and verify that this is indeed the case.

In Deuteronomy 4:13-14 Moses explains that God himself deliberately and clearly made a distinction between the Ten Commandments and all the other laws he gave, the former comprising the covenant made with his people, the latter being laws Moses was to teach to regulate their national life.

Think first of *how* the Ten Commandments were given and the place they occupied. Of all the laws given by God to the people through Moses, the Ten Commandments alone were engraved on the two tablets of stone (Exodus 34:28). Their having to be written a second time (Deuteronomy 10:4) because Moses broke the first tablets (Exodus 32:19; 34:1) emphasises their inviolable importance. Furthermore, they alone comprised the terms of the covenant between God and his people (Deuteronomy 4:13) and were encased in the ark of the covenant (Deuteronomy 10:5). They alone were thus housed in the place representing the presence of God on earth, in the holy of holies in the tabernacle (Exodus 25:21-22; 30:6). Their giving alone was accompanied by fire and earthquake and visible manifestations of the presence of God (Deuteronomy 4:9-14; 5:4). At the giving of the Ten Commandments the LORD spoke from heaven and the people heard his voice (Deuteronomy 5:4,22).

Thus everything about the manner in which the Ten Commandments were given, as well as what was said of them, distinguishes them from the rest of the laws which were given to the nation.

Think next about the *content* of the Ten Commandments compared with that of the other laws, and again a clear distinction is apparent. Whereas the ceremonial laws and the civil laws very specifically related to the religious and civil conduct of Israel as a nation, the Ten Commandments did not. There is a clear universalism of application in the Ten Commandments. That is, there is nothing about them which suggests they are limited to any particular people in any particular time … except for the fourth, perhaps? Very well, suppose we leave aside the fourth of these for a moment. Then there is certainly nothing exclusively Israelitish about the other nine. Even the Fifth Commandment, though it refers to living long 'in the land which the LORD your God is giving you', extends beyond the Israelite nation, for Paul applies it to Gentiles as well as Jews (Ephesians 6:3), asserting that the promise attached to it concerns their wellbeing and their living long *on the earth*. (Although the same Greek word serves for *land* and *earth*, the presence or lack of a qualifying word or clause indicates the geographical extent intended. For this reason there can be no doubt about what Paul is saying here.) So, though the promise as originally given to the Jews spoke in terms of the blessings *they* would enjoy in the land God was allotting to *them*, Paul is showing us that the language was contextualized, and that the promise was in fact universal in its scope. Honouring one's parents was not a commandment intended to be restricted to the Jews; neither was the promise accompanying it!

As far as the second section of the law is concerned, disrespect of parental authority, murder, adultery, theft, perjury, and covetousness are even now still generally recognized as destructive of a wholesome society if allowed free rein. It is ironic that in many so-called 'advanced' societies vast amounts of public money are spent endeavouring to redress the ills consequent upon conduct which is in breach of these commandments. Yet no matter how much money may be poured in, these ills cannot be put right unless and until the commandments are honoured. The commandments are not only universal, they are exclusive. That is to say, there is no way round them, there is no 'alternative therapy' by which men and women may live and thrive. People have been looking for long enough and are still looking; but they will search in vain!

Still thinking of the last six of the Ten Commandments, we note that when the rich young ruler came to Jesus, Jesus referred him to them (Mark 10:19). He said to him: 'You know the commandments: 'Do not commit adultery,' 'Do not murder.' 'Do not steal,' 'Do not bear false witness,' 'Do not defraud,' 'Honour your father and your mother'.' (Incidentally, when he said 'Do not defraud' he was indeed referring to the Tenth Commandment, for defrauding another is the direct consequence of covetousness.) Was Jesus speaking to the young man *as a Jew* or as a member of the human race? Of course, the young man, being a Jew and having the Ten Commandments, would have known that it was by keeping them that he would live. Leviticus 18:5 reads thus: 'You shall therefore keep my statutes and my judgements, which if a man does, he shall live by them.' By this the man understood in particular the Ten Commandments, and as the narrative continues it turns out that he was disappointed in his expectations, for he, though he thought he had kept the law, knew that he still lacked what he was looking for.

However, Jesus was not speaking to him simply as a Jew, but as one who *knew* the law and had certain expectations of it, for Jesus had said to him, 'You *know* the commandments....' So Jesus was addressing him as a Jew insofar as he *knew* the commandments, but not as a Jew insofar as the question was about eternal life. The *question* was not exclusively a Jewish one. The *standards* for eternal life (note that I am not saying the *means for obtaining* eternal life) are indeed enshrined in the law, and Jesus quoted to the man what was relevant to the case. The unfolding narrative reveals what the young man had not anticipated: that he had *not* kept the law.

Paul in Romans 1 and 2 indicates that the law—by which he means, as he explains, the moral law in the Ten Commandments—is as applicable to the Gentiles as it is to the Jews. We might note also that God judges the nations by the same standards as he judges the Jews, by his righteous laws, as prophecies against the nations confirm.

More could be said, which would only confirm that everything tells us that these commandments—or at least the last six—are of universal application, even though they were given in the first instance to the Israelite nation and only they entered into covenant with God to keep them. So we have disposed of the last six commandments and accept their validity.

Let us therefore come now to the first part of the law, the first four commandments. If the second part refers to our relationship with our fellow men and women, the first refers to our relationship with God. As Christians, how do we see the first three of these? Knowing the Lord, do we not understand the meaning of having no other gods before him? And not making and bowing down to carved images? And not abusing his name? Of course we do! We would not for a moment question the validity for us of these three commandments. Furthermore, because of what they are there is no question about their universal validity. So we have disposed of the first three commandments and accept their validity also.

This leaves, then, the fourth commandment: 'Remember the Sabbath day, to keep it holy.' If we are going to argue in the light of all that has been said thus far that this alone of all the ten is no longer binding, we must have very sound reasons for so doing. Remember what we are dealing with here: the holy law of God, nothing less. Remember the awe that fell upon the people to whom it was first given. Let us treat these words with the greatest of care. If the Fourth Commandment is no longer binding, let us have the clear authority of the Giver to tell us so. 'Why, Lord, have you placed a temporary law in this way among the rest which are so clearly permanent?'

Consider again Mark 2:27. The Sabbath was made for whom? For man. For the Jews? Yes. For the Jews only? No. For man. Thus the Sabbath has a bearing upon men whether they are Jews or not.

Suppose someone asks you, 'Precisely what does it mean, 'You shall not take the name of the Lord in vain'?' This is the third Commandment, and we should be able to give an explanation of its meaning in straightforward terms to anyone who asks us about it. The same applies to nine of the ten. The point particularly to note about the Ten Commandments is their straightforwardness. They are not difficult to understand, and their meaning is clear enough, although admittedly some have too shallow a view of them (remember Jesus' interpretation of some of them in the Sermon on the Mount, and his exposure of the young man's inadequate understanding of them, which we were considering a moment ago). These laws were not intended to be understood only by people with theological degrees: they were given originally to ordinary Jews. Now we come to the Fourth Commandment and ask the same question: 'Precisely what does it mean, 'Remember the Sabbath day, to keep it holy'?' Can you give a clear and concise answer to this without 'hemming and hawing'?

Let us now go over some of this ground again. *By* whom were the Ten Commandments given? They were given by God. *To* whom were they given? They were given to the Jewish nation through Moses. *Upon* whom were they binding? They were binding upon the Jews. Only upon the Jews? How do you answer? We must look at the context in which they were given. The people had been delivered from slavery in Egypt, and this was the formal constituting of the nation. This was *their* constitution. These laws were to regulate their behaviour, their conduct, their national life, *as the people of God*, for God had said, 'I am the LORD *your* God' (Exodus 20:2). We have laws in our land to regulate our conduct as members of the United Kingdom, and these are the ultimate reference for what is permissible and what is not in our personal, social and business affairs as they affect the state. Well, the Ten Commandments were given to a people whom God chose out to be *his* people, and were the ultimate reference for what was or was not permissible in terms of their relationship to *him*. I wish to emphasise that they were not given to the nation because they were Jewish, or because they were descendants of Abraham by a certain line, but primarily because they were called out to belong to God.

There are some who take the line that whereas the Fourth Commandment was given to Old Testament people, since the coming of Christ into the world and the establishment of the New Testament church and the gospel era this commandment now extends to seven days in seven, not just one. What a wonderfully spiritual concept this is! The trouble is, it won't stand up to scrutiny! How can the fallacy of this argument be exposed? Let me put to you a simple question: What were the Israelites supposed to do on the other six days? They were supposed to do all their work. That is what the Fourth Commandment says! So when do Christians do all *their* work? 'Oh, but', someone says, 'this command is about our relationship with God, and in Christ it has been restored onto a new footing which did not exist in Old Testament times. The Fourth Commandment was prophetic, pointing to the reconciliation Jesus would effect in dying on the cross for us, and now every day is like a Sabbath for us because we are now in fellowship with God through his Son.'

In answer to this, it must be understood (though often it is not) that there is *no* difference in status between a New Testament believer and an Old Testament believer. For example, King David's relationship with God was no different from yours or mine, and yet he was expected to keep the Sabbath! I am not suggesting his *knowledge* was the same, or that his *understanding* was the same, for there in some respects we have the advantage of him, living as we do at the end of the ages. But his *status was* the same. In God's eyes he was no less saved than you or I are saved. It was the same grace at work in his heart, by the same Holy Spirit, as we know and rejoice in. I have just stated that the Ten Commandments were given to the people of God *as the people of God*, and that they were to be regulative in their lives *as the people of God*. The spiritual Israelite, who enjoyed the same status before God that you and I enjoy through faith in Christ, had these commands to regulate his or her conduct in relationship with God and man. Can you picture for a moment the super-spiritual Israelite, seeing the tremendous significance of the Fourth Commandment, saying that the time was coming when it would apply to seven days in seven? The whole thing is ludicrous. This kind of thinking about the Fourth Commandment arises from a faulty concept of its meaning and purpose.

Taken as a whole, the law given to the nation of Israel was to be seen as of greater than national importance. In carefully keeping it, those to whom it was given would be distinguished as 'a wise and understanding people', a people to whom God was near and upon whom they could freely call (Deuteronomy 4:6-8). Had Israel carefully kept it, the law would have been a testimony to the perfection of the God who gave it. It expressed what he was like, what he required of his people, and what he has planned for them in his purposes of salvation. He had not given them his laws because they were Jews, but because they were to be his people.

Law versus grace?

One of the problems some people have with the Ten Commandments is that they seem to think that Old Testament believers were under law and

New Testament believers are under grace, and that there is therefore a fundamental difference between them. However, there is *no* such difference, because it is simply not true that Old Testament believers were under law and New Testament believers are under grace. Those who suggest there is a difference do so because they fail to appreciate the difference between law and grace and their respective spheres of operation.

The simple, straightforward answer to the question, 'Precisely what does it mean, 'Remember the Sabbath day, to keep it holy'?', is that God gave one day in seven for a special purpose. That purpose I have more than hinted at, and shall further expand later. It is nonsense to say that the Old Testament believer had only one day in seven, whereas the New Testament believer has seven days in seven, for fellowship with God.

I contend, therefore, that those who argue for a discontinuity at the Fourth Commandment do so on insufficient evidence. Their case fails to carry the weight of authority which would be essential in view of both the manner in which the Ten Commandments were given and the nature of their content. It is more likely that their supposed evidence is suspect than that the Sabbath has in any way been abrogated. I also contend that those who make a special case of the Fourth Commandment have actually failed properly to understand it. It is because they have failed properly to understand it that they find difficulty with it and so try to find a way round it. There is a sense in which the commandment which some have sought to remove from the statute book (or stone) is arguably the most important for the believer. Unwittingly they are doing themselves the greatest disservice possible by discounting what is in reality of greatest value to them, and it has arisen simply through failing to understand the commandment.

God never intended his laws to be followed mindlessly or slavishly. Servile obedience is not really obedience at all. If we are to understand his laws we need to ask why they were given and what they are there for, not with the intention of finding loopholes through which we may slip to avoid obedience because we don't want to keep them, but rather in order that we may render true and faithful obedience, pleasing to him. Jesus severely upbraided the Pharisees about the way in which they 'got round' the law over gifts supposedly 'devoted to God' (Mark 7:9-13) which in reality served only as a means of lining their own pockets and building their own little empire. Two noteworthy points come out of the confrontation. The first is the way Jesus by implication teaches something of the extent of the Fifth Commandment—that honouring one's parents includes providing for them according to their needs. The second is that if there is any apparent contradiction between the commandments then they are being either misunderstood or misinterpreted. If honouring God (which is implicit in all the commandments and which the Pharisees were purporting to be doing in this case) comes into conflict with honouring one's parents, it follows that something is wrong either with our understanding or with our motives. In the case of the Pharisees it would seem that they understood well enough, and that their consciences convicted them about their motives, for Jesus called them hypocrites. They covered the lie with layers of plausibility because to acknowledge it would have cost them too dearly.

Now it is sadly true that within the church there are some who find a conflict, not maybe among the commandments, but between law and grace, as if in some way they were diametrically opposed to each other. This is not to accuse such people of hypocrisy: they really are genuinely perturbed by the matter. They are afraid that if too much is made of the law it will discredit the grace of God. Somehow they do not seem able to come to terms with the fact that it is a gracious God who gave the law in the first place. So as far as the law is concerned they hedge it about with 'ifs' and 'buts' to the limiting of its scope and application. One sometimes gets the impression that it is an embarrassment to them. The law is there, 'but' we are now under grace, as if to say we ought now to have grown out of the law, or that it ought to be relegated to the archives. Yes, there is the law, 'but' we now have a better principle of life to govern us, and we are to be led by the Spirit. Why does a conflict of this kind exist in the minds of some people? The answer is that they are misunderstanding or misinterpreting the Word of God. Ironically, they are falling into exactly the same trap that those were whom Paul had to address in Romans and Galatians. The conflict did not lie within the Word of God, but arose out of their defective understanding of it. There is an essential harmony between the Old and New Testaments.

It is a great pity that so many people think of the Old and New

Testaments in terms of dichotomy and not unity, in terms of change and not continuity, in terms of obsolescence and not fulfilment. They think that the Old Covenant was characterized by imperfection and so had to be thrown out when Christ came and introduced the New.

But doesn't Hebrews 8:8 clearly imply that the first covenant was faulty? 'For if that first covenant had been faultless, then no place would have been sought for a second.' This is another example highlighting the necessity of understanding a statement in the context of the whole argument. The writer is not suggesting that the first covenant was fundamentally *flawed*. His whole argument through the chapters in which this statement is embedded is that the structure of the Old Covenant had run and served its purpose until the coming of Christ and, being a shadow of better things, gave way to the reality when Jesus completed his earthly ministry. The so-called 'fault' with it lay in the use people were trying to make of it. The law was never intended as a means of salvation. As the writer says at 7:19, 'The law made nothing perfect; on the other hand, there is the bringing in of a better hope, through which we draw near to God.' This is where the writer is finding fault with it. It is only faulty in respect of what it was never made to do! If I try to cut glass with a knife and fail, blunting the knife in the effort, I may find fault with the knife. If the knife had not been faultless, then no place would have been sought for a glass-cutter! The knife was perfect for what it was intended to do, but not beyond that. The illustration falls down, of course, because the Old Covenant actually pointed to the new in a multitude of pictorial ways. To say that the Old Covenant was a prototype of the New is also defective, because that suggests that the new does the same as the old only better. But the great danger of defective thinking in respect of the relationship between the Old and New Testaments is to conclude that the Old now has nothing regulative to tell us and therefore to relegate its teaching to the scrap heap. Whereas the fact is that not only does the New Testament quote extensively from the Old, but most of the teaching for the early church came directly from it, and the Lord's teaching and that of his apostles built upon the same secure foundation.

On whether the Ten Commandments are binding (to use an evocative word) upon the believer, it is all very well for some to say that we no longer need the law, but the fact is that we do need it, because we are still sinners. But doesn't God's Word say that Christ is the end of the law to those who believe? No, it does not. Romans 10:4 says that Christ is the end of the law *for righteousness* to everyone who believes! (It is perhaps not translated as clearly as it might be in the NIV.) This refers to how righteousness is to be obtained, and it is not by law. It says nothing about the applicability of the law in the life of the believer. In Galatians we are told that we as believers are not under the law, and that we have been redeemed from such a position (4:5). But neither are we above the law. The argument indicates that we have been brought into a totally new relationship with the law through faith in Christ, that it is we who have been changed.

In writing about the law Paul is at pains to show that it is holy (Romans 7:12). This has not altered. We cannot yet throw the law book out of the window and say it is irrelevant for us. A moment's serious reflection should suffice to make us aware of the folly of such an attitude. How (to take Paul's example) are we to know that there is really anything wrong in covetous thinking (Romans 7:7)? There's no harm in it, we might suppose as we give free rein to our imaginations while window shopping or surfing the internet or comparing what we have with others' possessions, adding to our list of 'must haves'! Indeed, the only way we really know that covetousness is wrong is because God has forbidden it. We will not find this prohibition anywhere else. Which is the very point the apostle is making. Even as Christians, we might justify it or excuse it as inconsequential, were it not for the fact that the law says otherwise. A similar line of thinking can be applied to others of the Ten Commandments. It is not only non-Christians who have self-justifying tendencies!

The Ten Commandments are just as applicable to us as they were to those who originally received them. We must never forget they were given to people in the context of redemption. In some ways they apply more to us than to unbelievers, for unquestionably they are *our* law! Redeemed by the precious blood of Christ, we are called to holiness (1 Peter 1:14-19), which means living in conformity to these commandments.

To be more specific and ask the question, 'Is the *Fourth* Commandment binding upon Christians?', the answer is unequivocally, 'Yes, it is.' To the question, 'Does the Fourth Commandment hold Christians in some kind of bondage?', the answer is emphatic: 'No, most certainly it does not!' It stands equally with all the other commandments in this respect. The law holds those in bondage who are *under* the law. It is those under the power of sin whose movements the law restricts, when it says 'You must do this' to those who don't want to do what it commands, and 'You mustn't do that' to those who do want to do what it forbids. The law rightly restrains such people from their lawless inclinations, acting as a rein upon their instinct to rush headlong into sin.

When the psalmist said, 'Oh, how I love your law! It is my meditation all the day' (Psalm 119:97), and when he said, 'Rivers of water run down from my eyes, because men do not keep your law' (verse 136) he was clearly not speaking as one above the law. As a redeemed man he had been changed in his relationship to the law. The law hadn't changed, but he had. The law which had been a tyrant to him was now his friend. For, redeemed by Christ (of whose work the sacrifices spoke in anticipation), he had been brought into reconciliation with God, and now loved God and his Word and his commands. If anyone dare go as far as saying that the law is no longer *binding*, it is most certainly regulative and we remain under its authority, and when we come to examine the matter more closely we may discover there is in fact little distinction. We are Christ's freedmen; we are also his bondservants, his slaves (1 Corinthians 7:22). What difference does it make if we regard ourselves as bound or free? We are his, and that is what matters.

Built-in obsolescence?

None of God's commandments have been superseded in the sense that we may now put them to one side and say they are no longer applicable or that they do not need to be considered. Before anyone protests, or contests this statement, I am not suggesting that animal sacrifices (for example) should still be made. The *practice* of such commandments has indeed been superseded, but we excise them from our consideration to the detriment of our appreciation of God's redemptive purposes and an adequate understanding of what the Lord Jesus accomplished upon the cross.

Let us consider one example of a ceremonial aspect of the law. The

Passover was to be celebrated annually by the Jews in remembrance of their deliverance from slavery in Egypt. Now surely this has been superseded? Indeed it has, and yet it has not been put to one side as if it no longer had any relevance. The Passover, though a single historical event, was nevertheless rich in prophetic symbolism, and when Jesus, in celebrating the Passover with his disciples in the upper room before his suffering and death said, 'This cup is the new covenant in my blood' (Luke 22:20), he was indicating that he was the real Passover lamb. When believers celebrate the Lord's Supper in remembrance of him, they are actually honouring the Passover law, recognizing its full significance in Christ and observing it accordingly. They do not celebrate the Passover in the way the Old Testament people of God did, because the manner of its celebration then was only partial and imperfect. In short, that law has not been abrogated or put to one side but is rather observed more perfectly in Christ who has fulfilled it ('Christ, our Passover, was sacrificed for us'—1 Corinthians 5:7).

An understanding of the Passover in the light of the sacrifice of the Lord Jesus Christ upon the cross helps us toward a deeper appreciation of what Jesus has actually accomplished for us there, shedding further light on the nature of redemption and the significance of substitutionary sacrifice.

The same argument applies to the many laws found in the Book of Leviticus. As we examine their meaning we are led into a more intimate understanding of what Jesus has done for us on the cross as 'the Lamb of God who takes away the sin of the world' (Matthew 26:28; John 1:29; Romans 3:23-26), and how he has served us, and does serve us, as our great High Priest. The Old Testament Jews who kept these particular laws did so by observing prophetic and typological ceremonies; the New Testament believers 'keep' these same laws in Christ as they bring into focus the work of redemption in all its various aspects. See Hebrews 9:13-15.

In Hebrews 10:9 we are told of Jesus taking away the first 'covenant' (9:18-20) in order to establish the second. The first was removed in order for it to be replaced by the second. What we must see is that it was not being replaced by something entirely different, but by something essentially the same only perfect. All the same elements were there, and they all spoke the same thing. It is difficult to find a suitable illustration to convey this point. A potential pilot may train using a simulator. The simulator helps prepare him for the real experience of flying and using the controls which actually do control the behaviour of the aircraft in the air. He may have some of the sensations of flying when sitting at the controls of the simulator, but he is not actually doing so. The simulator is there to prepare him for the real thing until the time comes when he is capable of doing it 'for real'. At the simulator, was he flying the aircraft or wasn't he? In a sense he was, in a sense he wasn't. It was all about the aircraft he was going to fly, but he wasn't actually flying it yet. However, when he is at the controls of the actual aircraft, it all has a familiar look to it, only this time it is the real thing.

Until the coming of Christ into the world his work had to be represented in some suitable way to prepare people for his coming. When he came and died on the cross and accomplished redemption's work, the significance of all that lay before was clearly apparent, but it had served its purpose, and now the worship was in the light of the body and not the shadow (Colossians 2:17).

Those who place the Fourth Commandment in this same category of having been fulfilled in Christ and superseded on account of his finished work, viewing it in ceremonial and typological terms (saying, for example, 'Christ is our rest'), have misunderstood it and failed to recognize its essentially moral aspect. The Ten Commandments, including the fourth, are moral commands because they address our responsibility toward God and our fellow men. The fourth in particular is concerned with the proper conduct of our relationship with God. It is therefore of a piece with the other nine and not, as some suppose, the odd one out. There is nothing remotely of a ceremonial nature in its requirements, and if anything this is emphasised by the fact that its observance extended to foreigners living in the land, who were excluded from all the ceremonial aspects of the national life of Israel.[4]

What is meant by 'the law'?

Where the term 'the law' is mentioned, particularly in the New Testament, what it means has to be understood from the context. It is important to understand this. For example, in the early chapters of Romans Paul has in mind different aspects of the law from what he writes about to the Galatians, for there is a difference in both emphasis and argument. Clearly there are common elements, but in Galatians he is dealing more with the ceremonial aspects of Judaism, whereas in Romans he is concerned rather with the moral element of the Ten Commandments. The writer to the Hebrews, on the other hand, is occupied largely with the ceremonial side of the law and its prophetic and typological character.

If many of the Ten Commandments are cast in negative form, why were they so given rather than their positive counterparts? The answer is simply because of sin. Were it not for man's natural sinfulness these commandments would not be necessary. It is precisely because sinful nature has a natural leaning to idolatry and murder and adultery and covetousness and the like that God had to say that these things can have no place in the lives of those in covenant relationship with him. So, 'You shall not commit adultery' indicates at once that God requires purity and faithfulness in the area of sexuality. The problem with the law is that it hits us where it hurts, as Paul illustrates in Romans 7:7-8. That is precisely what it is intended to do, as Paul again explains in Galatians 3:24.

God did in fact give his people his law simply and clearly in its positive aspects—Deuteronomy 6:5; Leviticus 19:18—but man's self-justifying tendency (Luke 10:29) and natural propensity to go in the opposite direction required this barrier to be set up.

That the law of commandments has not been done away with may be proved from Romans 13:8-10, where he says: 'Owe no one anything except to love one another, for he who loves another has fulfilled the law. For the commandments, 'You shall not commit adultery,' 'You shall not murder,' 'You shall not steal,' 'You shall not bear false witness,' 'You shall not covet,' and if there is any other commandment, are all summed up in this saying, namely, 'You shall love your neighbour as yourself.' Love does no harm to a neighbour; therefore love is the fulfilment of the law.'

The law fulfilled is not the law abrogated. He speaks here both of the law being 'fulfilled' and its being 'summarized' or 'summed up', which *per se* indicates it is still in force. Notice that Paul here refers to what is commonly called the second table of the law concerning our relationships with others. Interestingly he omits specific mention of the Fifth Commandment.

However, he does refer to it in Ephesians 6:1-3 where, again interestingly, his reference to it is in expansion of the summary statement of 5:2. 'Walk in love', he says, or, 'Live a life of love', and he explains what he means by alluding to a number of the Ten Commandments, which you may pick out from chapters 4, 5 and 6.

Concerning the law, then, both the summary and the expanded form have their place. The summary helps us not to miss the wood for the trees. The detailed version helps us when it comes to particulars. The back cover of a book may give us a summary of what the book is about, but that doesn't render the inside obsolete! The intention rather is to encourage us to look into it. If the law and the prophets hang upon the two great commandments of loving the Lord and loving our neighbour (Matthew 22:36-40) we are not therefore to conclude that the law and the prophets have nothing to say to us, but rather we should be encouraged to examine the matter further. The two great commandments were around at the same time as the law and were included in the body of the law. For example, in Deuteronomy 6:5 we find the first great commandment, and yet it is immediately followed by injunction carefully to keep *all* the commandments. There was no question of the superiority or inferiority of the one or the other. They said the same thing in different ways for different purposes. Nobody would question the ongoing validity of the two great commandments. As they are a summary of the Ten Commandments, it follows that the latter are as valid today as when they were first given.

Sinful human nature usually wishes to restrict the application of the law or to make out that it means something other than what it actually says. This, surely, is part of the reason why in the Sermon on the Mount Jesus expanded on some of the commandments (Matthew 5:17-48). In the light of this it is rather incongruous to hear some arguing that because Jesus came to fulfil the law (verses 17-18), the law of commandments, or at least parts of it, have ceased to apply since his death and resurrection. It is a manifest misunderstanding of his statement in these verses. By contrast, far from thinking to restrict the law's application, the writer of Psalm 119 sought to search out and explore its full extent, exclaiming with wonder in verse 96 on the extensiveness and perfection of the commandments.

Why was the law given?

We must face the uncomfortable truth. The covenant of promise given to Abraham already stood and was valid, but the law, Paul says, was 'added', giving the reason that it was 'because of transgressions' (Galatians 3:19), and he continues by explaining that the promise *given* to Abraham was actually *made* to Christ, and was effected through Christ. Paul does not say that the law was added until his coming, but that it was added *because of transgressions until his coming*. Christ did not come to deal with the law, but to deal with transgressions! The law, added because of sin and to expose sin, was there to lead transgressors to Christ (Galatians 3:24). It still serves the same purpose!

Why, or how, does the law expose sin? Our failure to keep the law makes it clear that we are transgressors of a standard God has set. But the law does much more than this. It is more than that we simply fall short of some arbitrary standard which has been set by another, as though it did not matter greatly whether we kept it or did not keep it. A household may impose certain rules upon its guests which are matters of convenience more than anything else, transgression of which may not in fact be of any consequence. God's rules are not like that. Our breach of them exposes us as *sinners*. We are made aware that something is actually wrong with *us* as well as deficient in our relationship with God.

So how does the law do this? It addresses our real problems by showing us God's righteous standards (note this again—righteous, not arbitrary). Consider a car which has been manufactured according to certain specifications and to perform according to certain standards. When it is taken for service it is subjected to a range of diagnostic tests. These tests have been provided by the manufacturer to determine whether or not the car is performing to the standard to which it was made. If it fails, the fault is not with the standard, it is with the car. It is malfunctioning, it is falling short of the standard. If it is not functioning as it ought because of abuse by the driver, the fault is not with the manufacturer, but with the driver.

Likewise God's law provides a diagnostic test of how we should be functioning, and if we fail at any point the only legitimate conclusion to be reached is that we are at fault, not performing according to the way our Maker intended, not according to the way we were made to perform. There is something wrong with *us*.

That this is so is clearly evident because lawlessness produces its own fruit which is both corrupting and destructive. Our lives have been driven in a fashion contrary to the Maker's instructions and it is therefore not surprising that the diagnostic fails us. We can blame neither the law nor its Giver. In just the same way as those suffering from an illness are usually uncomfortably aware of the fact, so those in breach of the law of God are usually aware that all it not well with them. In other words, they have not only the external witness of the law against them, but also internal testimony corroborating the fact.

To say that we no longer need the law now we are under grace is equivalent to saying that we are not sinners. Because the law was added because of transgressions, as long as we are sinners we need its corrective influence. The law of love is a high ideal and indeed a biblical one (Romans 13:8; Galatians 5:14; James 2:8; 1 John 4), but it must never be thought of as having no connection with the law of commandments. For example, in Romans 13:8 just referred to, Paul makes mention of the second table of the Ten Commandments by way of explanation of what is meant by the love which he urges upon his readers! It is sad that so many Christians in leadership, particularly in our modern permissive society, have fallen badly through neglect of the law of God. Let it be repeated: We may not be under law, but we are not above it either! Our relationship with the law of God should be that expressed by the psalmist in Psalms 19 and 119. These psalms express the effect the grace of God in us has in the way it totally transforms our attitude to the law. If the law is put in our minds and written on our hearts (Jeremiah 31:33) it stands to reason that it must be very much present in our lives! Christians need to maintain a healthy fear of the law of God, having it before their eyes always to remind them of their continuing need of forgiveness and of the abiding faithfulness of a gracious God (1 John 2:1).

There is also a lack of effectiveness in much preaching through neglect of the law because without it only part of the truth is being presented. All men will be judged on the basis of God's perfect standard of righteousness which is summarized in these commandments. However, surely the greater judgement will fall upon those who received the law and promised to keep it but failed to do so, than upon those who never knew it or, if they did, made no such promises of obedience? The writer to the Hebrews indicates much the same thing for those who have been brought under the blessings of the gospel but spurn the gracious Giver (10:26-31). In every way the imperative remains for us to ensure we are neither deceiving ourselves nor being deceived, and the only way this can be done is to measure ourselves against objective standards. This we do not that we may satisfy ourselves that we have attained a sufficient mark out of 10 in order to pass the test. Rather, it should be that we may recognize by our failure to reach the mark our continuing need for dependence upon the One who never failed to reach it, and to seek by his help to live to please him.

As long as we are sinners, we need the law written in stone as well as on our hearts. To dispense with the former on account of the latter is presumption. The law may no longer condemn us, but it will still convict us of sin. The work of the Holy Spirit is to testify of Christ, and the law is our tutor to lead us to Christ. This is not simply a once-and-for-all work when we become Christians, but a continual one as in the Christian life we are subject to trials and temptations. 'Prone to wander, Lord, I feel it, prone to leave the God I love; take my heart, O take and seal it, seal it from thy courts above' (Robert Robinson). Sometimes we need the stick of the law to make us smart under its correction that we may better appreciate the balm of God's love.

Returning to the Fourth Commandment, too many people, including many Christians, have a negative view of the Sabbath, thinking only in terms of its prohibitions and being fettered by them. They do not think to ask why a *loving* God should have given the Ten Commandments. Seeing the way the terms of the Fourth Commandment appear to restrict their activities, instead of thinking that their way of life needs attention, they look for ways around the commandment. Failing to recognize the problem lies with them, they find the commandment burdensome, which of course it is not (1 John 5:3).

John in this first letter refers more than once to the commandments. What does he mean by this? What commandments? Is he speaking in a non-legal way? Is he referring to things Jesus said, or does he include in his thinking the Ten Commandments? To make a dichotomy of this kind is totally artificial. There should be no division, because the position of Christians in relation to the law has changed. The law has not changed: it is we who have changed. It is with us just as it was with the psalmist which we noted earlier. When the psalmist speaks of his love for the law (Psalm 119:97), we cannot respond by saying that such sentiments do not apply to us as Christians. We cannot argue that now we are under grace the psalms which extol the law have little to say to us. Quite the opposite: as Christians we should understand just how much they do say to us! So, concerning the Sabbath, our problem with it, if we have a problem, is with us, not with the commandment. Putting our theological perspective aside for a moment, if we find the idea of one day in seven spent in the way the commandment prescribes in any way irksome, then there is something wanting in our Christian lives. Without mincing matters, it indicates to us that our fellowship with God and with his people is not what it ought to be. We may *say* we are walking with the Lord, but our irritation at the restrictions of the Sabbath tells a different story. 'When we walk with the Lord, in the light of his Word, what a glory he sheds on our way! While we do his good will, he abides with us still, and with all who will trust and obey! Trust and obey! For there's no other way to be happy in Jesus but to trust and obey' (John Henry Sammis). When we do so, we truly find the Sabbath to be a delight (Isaiah 58:13). We will return to the ongoing significance of the Sabbath when we come to a consideration of Hebrews 4.

In Exodus 20 there is the command to *remember* the Sabbath day. Once again, this clearly points to the very real possibility of its being neglected. Man as a sinner is for ever negligent of the Word of God, having an innate propensity for putting it to one side. The Israelites displayed this tendency even at the time of the law being given. The Sabbath was to be remembered by keeping it holy. I have already discussed the meaning of this. To get the force of the command to 'remember' you could use a concordance and look at some of the many places in which it is used in the Bible. We often think of remembering as resulting from what we had for a while forgotten—so that we forget first and remember afterwards. What is enjoined upon us in this command is rather different: we are to remember first so that we do not forget afterwards! To remember here means bringing the meaning of the Sabbath to mind and so meditating upon it that its truth becomes indelibly etched upon our thinking.

Leviticus 19:1-4 mentions the Sabbath in an interesting way. Indeed, the chapter itself is interesting, returning to the moral law after many chapters on ceremonial observances. Chapter 18, in dealing with laws about sexual morality, covers the seventh of the Ten Commandments. Chapter 19 first takes Commandments 5, 4, 1 and 2 in verses 3-4, then Commandments 8 and 9 in verses 11, 16, and Commandment 3 in verse 12. The sixth Commandment is covered in verse 17 as is clear when compared with Matthew 5:21-22. The chapter includes ceremonial elements, but the emphasis is upon righteousness and justice impartially maintained according to the absolute standards God has set, with the apposite caution of verse 15.

Of the Sabbath, though (verse 3), the command to keep it is uttered in the same breath as revering one's parents: 'Every one of you shall revere his mother and his father, and keep my Sabbaths: I am the LORD your God.' It is all part of the holiness God enjoins on his people, that they should be like him: 'You shall be holy, for I the LORD your God am holy' (verse 2), in which matter he has no problem with linking the honouring of one's parents with the keeping of the Sabbath. He seems to be saying that these two commandments fall into the same category in some respect, that they are of the same kind. Perhaps it is that in honouring one's parents one is acknowledging what one owes to them and that they justly have some claim upon their children; and likewise in keeping the Sabbath one is acknowledging what one owes to God and his just claim upon his children. These two commandments are vitally concerned with relationships and the spheres in which they operate. The Sabbath is all about our relationship with God. Put like this, these two commandments stand or fall together.

In all that we have considered thus far concerning the nature and purpose of the Sabbath, there has not been the least hint of potential obsolescence. In fact, the very opposite is the case, for everything about it seems to point to its abiding relevance.

There is something further which should be said about the Ten

Commandments in order for us to see the fourth in its proper light, and that is that the commandments were given to God's covenant people and not to humanity in general. I hinted at this earlier when I said they were given to the nation *as the people of God.* This is not for a moment to deny that they are universal in their application or to suggest that God does not require the same standard of righteousness of all mankind. But the focus here is on the people God owns as his, and the giving of the Ten Commandments is set in the context of redemption, as Exodus 20:2 makes clear—'I am the LORD your God, who brought you out of the land of Egypt, out of the house of bondage. You shall have no other gods before me' etc. They were given to a people who had been delivered from slavery under a tyrannical master in order that they might belong to another Master. The Ten Commandments were not given to impose a new tyranny in place of the old. They indicated the framework in which redeemed man could work out his relationship with God and with his fellows; and although many of them are stated in negative form, there is a comprehensiveness about them which leaves no area of life untouched. The *problem* with the law occurs only *outside* the context of redemption. The psalmist could speak of the law in glowing terms (Psalms 19 and 119 again) because he viewed it through the eyes of one who had been saved. The Ten Commandments were not given to be prophetic or symbolic as were the ceremonial laws. They were not given for a time only, to be superseded by something better. They are now what they always were. When originally given it was made abundantly clear that they were distinct from any of the ceremonial or civil laws. Because they were given as a basis for man's relationship with God and his fellow men they are as meaningful today as they were in Moses' time, and no exception is to be made in respect of the Fourth Commandment.

When the Sabbath was built into the Ten Commandments it was given as the last part of what is usually called the first table of the law. The Ten Commandments can truly be kept only in the context of redemption. That is why when people aim for justification by means of keeping the law they fail. But in the context of redemption, we see God first (Commandment 1), God alone to be worshipped and served (Commandment 2), with no perversion in the form of misrepresentation (Commandment 3). The culmination of the requirements of the first three commandments lies in the fourth, because this is the practical outworking of man's relationship with God. The Fourth Commandment, which so many despise or would seek to do away with, is actually pivotal to all the commandments, because it is there to safeguard the heart of man's relationship with God, out of which all other things flow.

Jesus said, 'If you love me, keep my commandments' (John 14:15); and, 'He who has my commandments and keeps them, it is he who loves me' (John 14:21); and, 'If you keep my commandments, you will abide in my love, just as I have kept my Father's commandments and abide in his love' (John 15:10). To love him is to please him, to please him is to obey him. Love is the fulfilment of the law, says Paul, quoting a number of the Ten Commandments (Romans 13:8-10). Love fulfils the law, it doesn't dispose of it—there is a world of difference!

A song for the Sabbath

The Holy Spirit has left on record that Psalm 92 is 'A song for the Sabbath day'.[5] It is worth asking why, for our attention is being drawn to the fact and it is the only psalm thus described. What are its features which make it particularly appropriate for the occasion, or what insight does it give about the nature and use of the day for the spiritually-minded believer? We have already noted from Leviticus 23:3 that the Sabbath was to be a day for God's people to assemble together for worship as well as its being a day of rest. There is nothing cold or formal in the language of this psalm. On the contrary, the sentiments expressed in it well up from a heart which is warm toward God with a sincere affection. The psalm shows its writer to be a happy man, finding his enjoyment and his joy in God, and it is fair to infer that this was intended to be a dominant feature of the Sabbath. We are looking at a man who knew from experience that this was a day of blessing to him, and that what God said about it and promised in connection with it was true.

When he says at the opening that 'it is good' to give thanks to God and praise his name, we are immediately introduced into what the Sabbath is all about. 'Here we are at another Sabbath, and I can put my work to one side and give myself to the worship of my God—it is good to be able to do so.' That is not to suggest that the psalmist did not praise the Lord at other times; only that this time was special, and he could do so without the distraction of other cares or responsibilities, given a time slot devoted exclusively for this purpose by God himself. 'This is good,' he says, and he is going to make the most of it!

Out come the musical instruments (verse 3) to assist the worshippers in their songs of praise. Mere words are insufficient in praise of God. There must be music, there must be vocalization in song to assist the expression of what is in the heart. If song is a fitting medium of praise and thanksgiving in heaven (see for example Revelation 5 and 15), it is hardly surprising that the redeemed should be practising now! One of the characteristics of such singing, though, is that it is chiefly a corporate activity. The people are doing it together, their voices combining both in unison and in harmony in worship. There is also a meditative aspect to good singing as it focuses the mind with the measured expression of the truths it expresses.

Sometimes the singing of songs can serve little better purpose than the stirring up of emotions, a mindless chanting of sentiment with little content. We see, though, that the songs which occupy the psalmist not only state, but also explore, the deep things of God. They are uttered neither to make the singer feel good nor to stir up his emotions (though they may actually result in both of these things), but primarily to enable him to express his worship of God in a meaningful and fitting way. In Colossians 3:16 the apostle Paul writes: 'Let the word of Christ dwell in you richly in all wisdom, teaching and admonishing one another in psalms and hymns and spiritual songs, singing with grace in your hearts to the Lord' (and he says much the same thing in Ephesians 5:19). What is particularly interesting about the way he puts it is that while we are singing with grace in our hearts to the Lord we are also instructing one another. Singing has this dual aspect: it is to the Lord, and it is at the same time to one another. Good songs which glorify God develop out of an intimacy with the word of Christ and are designed to build up the church. If both of these aspects are not present the singing certainly does not fall into the category which the Word of God approves.

As for the details and the timing of the events of the day, little is said. Some people go to church in the morning and again in the evening, but what they do in between seems to have little to do with either event! Verse 2 is not to be taken in that sort of way! It has been suggested that the psalmist had in mind the times for the offering of the morning and evening sacrifice when people would gather together for worship. (Numbers 28:3-10 refer to these offerings which were made every day, including the Sabbath.) However, the way he puts it militates against this idea, for he writes not of morning and evening but of morning and night, a word which is not, and cannot be, used for the time of the evening sacrifice. So even though there were both a morning and an evening sacrifice on the Sabbath, as on any other day, this verse is not so much marking two distinct events as indicating the beginning and ending of a single event. Taken in its context, it is a poetic device to indicate that the whole day is taken up with the things of God. By 'morning' is indicated the commencement of the day's activity, while 'night' lies beyond the evening into the time when the day is truly over and nothing further can be done.

There is something delightful about the terms the psalmist uses in verse 2. The day opens with 'God is love.' Actually it is more than that. He declares that God is love because, as the word in the original indicates, God has shown his love to him, for this is the covenant love bestowed by the LORD upon his elect children. What wife can truly say her husband loves her if he rarely gives her his time and attention? The very fact that God has given the day for quality time with him indicates to his people that he is a God of love. His people know that he loves them, and they are glad to take this opportunity to declare it. But by the time the end of the day arrives, the song is now of God's faithfulness. God is true to his word. He not only declares his love, he also demonstrates it; he not only makes promises, he also keeps them. The fact that the psalmist can so speak—or rather sing—at the close of the day indicates something of what has happened in the intervening hours, and verses 4-5 hint at what this is. The gladness, the joy, the wonder expressed here are the product of meditation on, not merely cursory attention to, the things mentioned. In particular, God's 'works' and his 'thoughts' are alluded to. The former seems to encompass the full range of his works, embracing creation, providence and redemption, and the latter his counsel as displayed in the outworking of his purposes.

As the psalmist dwells upon these things he bows his intellect to the infinite superiority of God's understanding and wisdom, whose thoughts and ways are so far above ours (Isaiah 55:8-9), in much the same way as the apostle Paul, after his analysis of the gospel and God's plan of salvation, bursts forth with the doxology of Romans 11:33-36. Only those who have had the privilege of spending time in God's presence, pondering his Word and waiting upon him, can really identify with the psalmist or the apostle in this. The Sabbath gave this precious opportunity.

Meditation upon the things of God—his works and ways—is a means of allowing time for these truths to enter and find suitable lodging in our brains. It is something the man in a hurry finds difficult, if not impossible. It is something the man or woman preoccupied with the affairs of this life—whether work or family matters or such like—simply cannot give time to. Things have not changed. That is why God gave his people the Sabbath. It gave them time for what was of supreme importance to them, so that they could get to know their God more fully. Not an hour in the morning and an hour in the evening, not a corner of time here or there as opportunity might be found, but an undivided day for an undivided purpose—that is what God has provided. Because God is infinite in all his attributes, this opportunity was an inexhaustible one, and so the weekly Sabbath was an appropriate provision for the purpose. Man needed to work, for that was built into the creation mandate (Genesis 1:28); but he also needed fellowship with God, which was also built into it, and this need was the greater after the entry of sin into the world.

One of the aids to meditation is instruction. The psalmist could not have written verses 4 and 5 unless he had acquired an understanding of God's works. He had learned about creation, he had learned about the history of God's dealings with his people, and he had learned about salvation. In order to learn, he had been instructed through the various means which had been available to him. For ourselves, if we are finding it difficult to identify with the sentiments expressed here by this man of God, it may be because our experience in this area falls short of his. For him the Sabbath provided a learning opportunity, when he could give time not only to singing the praise of his God, but also to furthering and perfecting that praise with a fuller understanding. Study and learning are not always welcome activities, especially when we find the subject dull or difficult. When it comes to the things of God, though, the mind of his people should be receptive when we appreciate the purpose of it all. We should relish the opportunity afforded us. The Sabbath was a God-given opportunity to learn of him and from him.

The final thing to note from this psalm for our purposes is that for the psalmist the Sabbath was a day to be spent in the house of the Lord (verse 13a) and in his courts (verse 13b). The tabernacle, and later the temple, symbolized the place on earth where God met with his people (Exodus 25:22; 29:42-44). The whole point about the Sabbath was for God's people to come into his presence and enter into all the benefits that such a meeting afforded. One of the ideas this psalm employs is that of 'flourishing' (verses 7, 12, 13), and a comparison is made between how the ungodly spring up and flourish, and how the godly do. The wicked spring up like *grass* (verse 7), which flourishes for a short while but soon withers and is cut down. They have neither substance nor value, for all their show.

The righteous, on the other hand, flourish like a palm tree and grow like a cedar of Lebanon, and continue fruitful into old age (verses 12-15), the secret being where they are planted and where they grow. The house and courts of the Lord are the place of birth and nurture and nourishment as far as the righteous are concerned; the place symbolic of the meeting of God with his gathered people. God is central to their lives, from which reference point they reach out to others, spreading their holy influence. The mention of the palm and the cedar of Lebanon is significant, for these were trees of importance. Palms are much valued and useful evergreens which grow where there is a good supply of fresh water, and the righteous grow where the life-giving influence of the Holy Spirit pervades. The cedar of Lebanon is a tree of unsurpassed magnificence and strength, the roots of which run deeply where it is planted, anchoring it securely, and it lives to a great age. The picture is of God's people rooted and grounded in him, established and unmoved, prominent and powerful in their testimony to his unfailing righteousness (verse 15).

We must remember that these things are what the psalmist saw in connection with the Sabbath day. It is only those who so valued and used their God-given privileges who could live like this and find lasting happiness and fulfilment in life through their drawing upon the riches God was pleased to lavish upon them as they honoured him upon this day, which he declared to be his day. They, and they alone, were the ones to remain strong, fruitful, fresh and green, and unshakable in their confidence in God.

From morning light till late at night,
this day of days we have the right
our God to praise, our voices raise
in thankful song—we who belong
to One whose love for us is strong
 and cannot fail, but must prevail—
 our faithful God, true to his Word.

Declaring thus with melody,
and strings' enriching harmony,
we trace the grace which made us free—
his tender power creating hearts
that beat with joy which he imparts:
 re-made through his life-giving Word
 and drawn to love our loving Lord.

The wonders of creation thrill
the minds of those who on them dwell.
We glory in his thoughts profound:
what he has made, what he has said,
what he upholds: whose woven thread
 of sovereign plan we may explore—
 God's wisdom without fault or flaw.

How foolish he whose mind is full
of selfish thought and therefore dull,
and cannot see (though plain to all
who fear the Lord and on him call),
that wickedness will have its day—
 but brief and short, soon swept away,
 forgotten with its dying ray.

Enthroned on high, God will destroy
all proud and poisonous enmity,
while lifting up his chosen ones,
infusing joy and strength, that they,
though trodden down, remain secure:
>*and if much scorn they must endure,*
>*they triumph in his victory.*

His people, planted by his grace
within this safe and blessed place,
will flourish, fresh and fruitful, while
even to aged years they still
his glory shall display, and tell
>*that all he does is good and right:*
>*our Rock and Refuge, sole delight.*

Contending for the Sabbath

In the Old Testament there are a number of allusions to God taking issue with the Israelites over their abuse of the Sabbath day. Before we look at these and try to see where the issue lay we should notice that at least in the periods of Israel's history covered by these incidents the Sabbath was recognized and observed. To what extent it was observed is another question, and how it was observed is the bone of contention between God and the people.

Amos and Israel

Historically first, we look at Amos 8:4-6. The New Moon was recognized as a day of rest like the weekly Sabbath. There are three things we can learn from this passage. Firstly, in the time of Amos, even in the northern kingdom of Israel where the worship of God was largely corrupted, the Sabbath appears to have been fairly rigorously observed, at least insofar as trade was not being undertaken. Secondly, the people against whom the charge was being made were much more interested in doing business and making money than in Sabbath observance, because clearly the Sabbath and any other 'holy day' were an inconvenience to them, their sole concern being to get them over as quickly as possible so that they could get on with what mattered most to them. Thirdly, these people who had such a low regard for the Sabbath were also unscrupulous in their business dealings, bending the rules and exploiting anyone and everyone, but especially the vulnerable, for the sake of personal gain.

When Amos quotes the people as saying, 'When will the New Moon be past, That we may sell grain? And the Sabbath, That we may trade wheat? Making the ephah small and the shekel large, Falsifying the scales by deceit, That we may buy the poor for silver, And the needy for a pair of sandals—Even sell the bad wheat', it is very much to be doubted whether anyone was actually uttering these words! Actions speak louder than words, and he was quoting what their actions said.

Amos could have made his point about riding roughshod over the underprivileged without reference to the Sabbath, omitting the first part of verse 5: 'Hear this, you who swallow up the needy and make the poor of the land fail, making the ephah small and the shekel large, falsifying the scales....' Well aware of the rampant corruption, he was going public and exposing the extortionate practices. However, the New Moon and the Sabbath got in the way of these people, and so in putting these words into their mouth Amos is exposing not only their deficient attitude toward their fellows but also their deficient attitude toward God.

We are, it seems, to draw the conclusion that he is saying as much about sharp practice concerning the Sabbath as sharp practice concerning business, and that the two are very definitely connected. The two great commandments go hand in hand—you can't have one without the other. Where the fear of God is left off, there begin greed, malice and covetousness (see Romans 1:29-31 for a fuller list!). We cannot love our neighbour as ourselves unless and until our hearts are tender toward God. Neither can we love God with all our heart, mind, soul and strength without it showing in compassion in our dealings with our fellow men and women. The charge Amos makes against these people is that they have departed from the fear of God. How is that evident? It is certainly evident in their corrupt dealings with their fellows; but it is supremely evident in their lack of esteem for the Sabbath. They have no use for the Sabbath because they have no time for God. Their observance of it, such as it was, was devoid of meaning.

The question, 'When will the Sabbath be over?' demonstrates that outward observance is not enough. They had a form of observance but not the spirit. Thus they abused it even while they observed it. It was just the same problem as when God said to the people of Judah through Isaiah that he abhorred their sacrifices (Isaiah 1:10-13). They had everything in place as far as religious observance was concerned. It wasn't the bringing of sacrifices that mattered but the manner in which they were brought. Sacrifice is no substitute for obedience (1 Samuel 15:22), and heartless obedience is not obedience at all. Paul reminds us that the same applies to the Lord's Supper. What the Corinthians thought they were doing was eating the Lord's Supper. But, Paul asserts, that is exactly what they were not doing (1 Corinthians 11:20). We honour God when our obedience results from a true recognition of his provision, not otherwise (1 Corinthians 11:29). In a nutshell, this is what obedience to the Ten Commandments is all about, and this has never changed.

There is something of an irony in that Amos was addressing the nation of Israel when they were enjoying an unusual period of peace and prosperity under Jeroboam II. The reason given by God for this is found in 2 Kings 14:26-27—'For the LORD saw that the affliction of Israel was very bitter; and whether bond or free, there was no helper for Israel. And the LORD did not say that he would blot out the name of Israel from under heaven; but he saved them by the hand of Jeroboam the son of Joash.' Not only did the Lord show his compassion in giving the people relief from their severe troubles, but in his mercy he sent his servant Amos, and others, to preach to them his word, giving them what turned out to be virtually a last opportunity for repentance. For in little more than a generation Israel was to be wiped off the map and assimilated into the Assyrian empire. The very respite which the nation was given by God for serious reflection was grossly abused. They were too comfortable to take much notice of Amos' warnings, too secure to begin to imagine that his predictions should be taken seriously, too preoccupied with the affairs of this world to find time for God when they considered they did not need him.

The tragedy of this chapter of 'final judgement' (verse 2) is not only that they would shortly be stripped of every material benefit, but also that they would be deprived of what actually mattered most: 'of hearing the words of the Lord' (verse 11). God, whom they had despised and ignored, had spoken his final word to them. No more would they hear from him (verse 12). If only they had taken Amos seriously … but they didn't! How often has this been repeated in history right down to our own day. If we are comfortable and at ease (compare Amos 6:1) it will be woe to us too if we fail to recognize from whom these benefits come and spurn the Giver.

Before leaving Amos it is imperative that we note again the principal symptom of degeneracy in his society. That one special provision the Lord had put in place for the safeguarding of their relationship with him, and the root from which every blessing flowed, they were squeezing out of their lives. Whatever view, reader, you take on the Sabbath issue, let it not be that your time for God is small and your time for business and material prosperity large.

Isaiah and Judah

Not many years later Isaiah, in chapter 58, took up the same issue, this time with the people of Judah in the south who perhaps were not quite as blatant in their attitudes as those of Israel in the north whom Amos had addressed, for they covered it with a veneer of orthodox religious respectability. This two-faced attitude he exposes in the opening verses. Please read the whole of the chapter. Outwardly in their attention to the propriety of their religious observances the people gave the impression of being upright and God-fearing (verse 2), and perhaps they themselves even thought they were 'doing all right', for they reproached God for apparently neither seeing nor heeding their fasting and therefore, presumably, for not answering their requests (verse 3a).

One cannot help thinking of the comparable attitude of many of the religious leaders of Jesus' time whom he so devastatingly exposed for their hypocrisy (Matthew 23). Such is the deceitfulness of sin that we can convince ourselves that we are pleasing God when in reality we are like smoke in his nostrils (Isaiah 65:5). How can you say you love God when you see your brother in need and do nothing about it (1 John 3:17)?

This is the acid test God puts to the people through his servant Isaiah, for as well as exposing their empty self-righteousness he shows that they are self-centredly insensitive to the needs of others (verse 3b). Neither tenderness nor compassion are to be seen here, only the brutal recognition of the need to look after the interests of 'number one' (verse 4). It is the survival of the fittest mentality in its ugliest manifestation of suppressing the aspirations of others and treading down rather than helping up those who are struggling, with the attitude of 'It's their hard luck; it's their problem; it's not my responsibility;' and, worse than that, 'I can use my power over them to keep them where they are and extract what I can from them for my own ends.' These things are all to be seen in this chapter. It is, in fact, little different from the way the Egyptians treated the Israelites during their years of slavery.

God, who had always shown himself to be compassionate and caring toward the deprived elements of society, intends and expects this same attitude to prevail among his people (for example, to take just a few references, Exodus 22:21-27; Deuteronomy 10:18-19; 14:29; 16:11-12; 24:19-

22; 26:12; 27:19; James 1:27). This principle lies at the core of the law, and is a practical expression of what is meant to love one's neighbour as oneself (Galatians 5:14). This chapter takes up the point in a big way, spelling it out to the people in unmistakable terms. Their attitude toward their neighbours was all wrong, for which reason they could not expect God's blessing upon them until these things were put right.

But there is more. For if we ask what all this has to do with the Sabbath (verse 13), we find that the prophet has been leading up to this point in his exposure of his people's sin. It wasn't that they really had been seeking God but needed some correction in the area of their relationship with their fellow beings. It wasn't that they needed to reform their lives in relation to their neighbours. Of course they did need to do that, but the point is that their relationship with themselves and with others was wrong because their relationship with God was wrong. Isaiah in Judah, like Amos before him in Israel, is showing that the two aspects are organically connected. A point made in connection with Amos bears repeating here, because God repeats it. When we observe that the law is summarized in two great commandments, 'You shall love the Lord your God with all your heart … and your neighbour as yourself' (Luke 10:27), these are not two separate commandments as if it might theoretically be possible to keep either without the other. Isaiah is pointing out that, contrary to outward appearances, the people's relationship with God was all wrong, and that it was proved by their neglect or exploitation of their fellows. Having spelt out what he means by this, he then returns to the matter of their relationship with God, the natural focus for which was in their observance of the weekly Sabbath.

Three questions

Here, in verses 13-14, Isaiah balances negative and positive aspects of Sabbath observance which we can consider through three questions connected with it which are implicit in the text: 'Where shall we go?' … 'What shall we do?' … 'What shall we talk about?'

The answers to these questions depend very much upon one's point of view. For those who viewed the Sabbath in terms of its prohibitions and saw them as a kill-joy and restrictive influence, the questions implicit in these verses would have been hard to answer. For them the Sabbath was anything but a delight: a dull and boring day bound with the necessities of religious duties, any legitimate relief from which was to be welcomed with both arms. If they must go to the temple and go through the motions (though they would much rather be elsewhere) they could at least endeavour to make it a profitable social occasion, catch up with the latest local gossip and do what they could to further their own interests during the week to come: in other words, turn a boring necessity into a useful opportunity. Then as a bonus they would have the satisfaction of having done their duty and feel better for it. Or had they...? Or would they...?

One of the features in this prophetic section of Isaiah's writing is that the sharp rebukes to the people are given in the context of rich promises in three declarations of the form 'If ... then...' Do look for them in this chapter. The first 'If' is presupposed in verses 6-7, for the prophet says, in effect, 'If you do these things, 'Then your light shall break forth like the morning..."' (verses 8-9a). The second pair is in verses 9b-12, and the third in verses 13-14.

If in each case you think about what it is which is promised, you will see that, if there is any allusion to material prosperity or health or peace or happiness, these things are couched in terms which make it very difficult for the worldly-minded person to understand or accept, for they are all about going on with God (verses 8b-9, 11, 14). Such a person wants these things without 'going on with God'. Isaiah is showing that they cannot be had! So, as is invariably the case, those who took exception to the prophet's words would have found nothing to encourage them in the 'then...' aspect of the rebukes. To them the promises of God would have meant nothing of substance. Like uncut diamonds they would have been viewed and discarded as worthless pebbles. The Word of God has always been treated like this by some. Yet it does not return to him void, as Isaiah himself has already said (55:11), and to those who took the rebuke to heart, recognizing that they deserved it and that things were wrong with their lives which needed to be put right—to them the promises of God would have begun to sparkle, revealing their true and incalculable worth. This is why God required of people who did not regard the Sabbath as a delight to call it a delight. The only way that could come about was through their humbling themselves before him and trembling at his word (Isaiah 66:2).

Many parents have known the embarrassment when dining out with friends of the food set before their children being refused or picked at distastefully, not at all because it is unwholesome but simply because it is unfamiliar to them. They will say they don't like it, not because they don't like it but because they think they won't like it!

'It's good for you!'

'Yes, but I'm not going to like it!'

It is always a relief when they get to the point of being willing to try something on its merit and discovering it is not as bad as at first appears. 'Wow!—this is really good ... can I have some more?' Adults are somewhat more sophisticated in prejudging situations and displaying a natural resilience to change.

How could people *call* the Sabbath a delight when they *considered* it to be anything but? This is typical of the dilemma people face when God's Word challenges sinful human nature. Only as we respond in humility and repentance, acknowledging that what God says of us is true, do we begin to find it to be as he describes it. We've first got to pick up the laden spoon and put it to our mouth instead of sitting there with defiant resistance! God said to his people that *they* were to call the Sabbath a delight, for that was what *God* called it. Calling it a delight, they would find it a delight, because, as he then promised, they would find themselves delighting in the Lord!

Likewise those taking to heart the strictures of the previous verses would find that the 'dubious' blessings promised would turn out to be real blessings indeed. Are you giving God short measure in your life? Then put him to the test and see if he is not as good as his word (Malachi 3:10)!

Now what about those three questions? First of all, 'Where shall we go?' 'If you turn away your foot from the Sabbath' indicates either that they were breaking the Sabbath by turning their feet in other directions (as in the NIV translation), or that metaphorically they were trampling all over the Sabbath. Practically, it makes little difference, for the meaning is clear enough. In Psalm 122:1 David is in no doubt as to where he wishes to turn his feet. We may talk of going to church; the Jews may have spoken of going up to the temple. How does David put it? His desire is to go to the house of the Lord. What makes church what it should be? What made the temple what it should be? The name of the Lord, the presence of the Lord. Before someone corrects me and points out (quite rightly) that the church is the people of God and not a building, what then *is* the answer to the question: 'What makes the church what it should be?'? It is exactly the same! Furthermore, it puts an edge on David's introduction, for he is not thinking to go alone! How it gladdens his heart that others are saying to him, 'Let *us* go into the house of the Lord,' and as he continues, speaking of '*our* feet … standing…'. Another Sabbath has come round. Where shall *we* go? Let us direct our steps to the place where we may meet with our God, where we may praise his name, where we may give thanks to him and pray to him. Let us go where God may be found among his people! Would your heart miss a beat from shock at the very thought of such a privilege being denied you? What is your view in this sin-weary world obsessed with *things*, of the opportunity of meeting with the people of God for worship, fellowship and instruction? God gave his people the Sabbath for this very purpose.

The next question, 'What shall we do?' has clearly already been partially answered. Isaiah (verse 13 again) upbraided the people from doing their pleasure on God's holy day. When we refer to people 'doing their own thing' it is usually an indication that they have made up their own minds as to what they are going to do without any particular reference to others, and off they go and do it. It is frequently a recipe for trouble when members of a family go off and 'do their own thing' without considering they have responsibilities toward the others in the family. How much more so when those whom God has called to belong to his family go off and do their own thing, thinking only of themselves without any consideration to what he wants beyond the notion that his requirements are restrictive and unreasonable. If it grieves an earthly father to see his children dishonouring him by doing their own thing contrary to his loving and wise advice and pleading, how do we imagine it grieves the Lord to see those called by his name going their own ways instead of honouring him—he who has given the Sabbath to be a delight, for his rightful honour and their unspilt blessing?

Further to answer the question, 'What shall we do?' we turn once more to the Psalms, this time to Psalm 95 which is poignantly connected with a later study in this book. Mention has already been made of going to where we may meet with God with praise, thanksgiving and in prayer. Praise is very much in the forefront of this psalm, with singing (verse 1) and thanksgiving—and even joyful shouting (verse 2, NKJV)!—in view of his greatness, power and glory. These things are right and proper and do indeed honour him. But lest we get caught up in all the activity of these things, let us observe that at the heart of this psalm is the call to worship God, our Maker (verse 6) and our Saviour (verse 1). The very call to 'Come' (verses 1, 6) proceeds from the heart of one who has been in the presence of the Lord. So when it comes to 'What shall we do?', we let the psalmist answer: 'O come, let us worship and bow down; let us kneel before the Lord our Maker. For he is our God, and we are the people of his pasture, and the sheep of his hand.' This is the language of intimacy, of reverence, of submission, and it is here first and foremost where we truly honour him. It is out of this vital relationship with him that all the visible, outward forms of worship take shape and have meaning. Without it, it is all empty form, and though we may be stirred emotionally by all that is going on, it will afterwards leave us deflated and disappointed and unable to meet the challenges of life. If he is your God, then guard the place of communion with him, remembering that it is by the blood of Jesus that you have access into his holy presence (Hebrews 10:19), and that by shedding his blood for you he has given you the right to be there. Think about that, and surely you will find within yourself a ready response to the psalmist's call!

'What shall we talk about?' is the third question to be addressed. The parallelism of the poetic structure of Isaiah 58:13 alludes to three areas in which God found fault with the people, and it concerned their own ways, their own pleasures, and their own words. They were self-centred in what they did, in what they found pleasure in, and in what they talked about. As with the two questions we have already thought about, we will let the Psalms give us the answer to this last one, too. For this we return to Psalm 92:2. 'It is good' says the writer, '...to declare your lovingkindness in the morning, and your faithfulness every night.' This was briefly touched upon earlier from the viewpoint of the worshipper. Let us now think of what it means from God's angle and how it affects us.

In referring to God's lovingkindness (love, NIV) the psalmist is thinking here of God's covenant love toward his people. It is a form of contract by which God has bound himself to love them—a contract into which they have been privileged to enter by his sovereign choice. We are rather familiar these days with marriage contracts in which the promises made by the partners are all too easily broken. Although the words of the promises made in the marriage ceremony indicate unconditional faithfulness the one toward the other, in practice they are all too often treated with contempt. Many a cynic, if not most, might say of the promises made by men that they are not worth the paper they are written on. Not so, thankfully, with God, or else where would we be? When we read over and over again in the Bible of God's covenant love we may be profoundly thankful that it is worth a great deal more than the paper it is written on! How many times do we prove ourselves to be unworthy of the love he has declared toward us? How often, between the rising of the sun and its setting do we have cause to regret our conduct and wonder how God could love us—or even, when things are particularly bad, whether we may dare hope he still loves us? Here we have our answer. Even if we are faithless, he remains faithful, for he cannot deny himself (2 Timothy 2:13).

Paul understood the meaning of God's covenant love. So did the psalmist. It was an understanding not in any way to excuse the abusing of his love (compare Romans 6:1) but to be profoundly thankful that God is true to his word. We might declare our love to God in the morning, and mean it ... but would we be able to speak of our faithfulness to our love that same night? I think not! This is nothing to sing about, rather something to lament. Do you see, believer, how precious is the truth enunciated here in the psalm? For the declaration is of *God's* love, and *his* faithfulness. We can say of God what can be said of no one else: he is utterly faithful to his word, and in particular to his covenant love. We are absolutely and completely dependent upon that. It is said that it takes two to make an argument. For our present purposes, it takes two to break a contract. If God were like us, it would not last the day. As it is, it will last for all eternity, because nothing can separate us from his love toward us in Christ (Romans 8:35-39). With confidence, therefore, we can declare his lovingkindness in the morning and his faithfulness at night. But more than with confidence: it is with profound thankfulness, for our eternal security is bound up in this truth.

In view of this, what are we to make of those whose primary interest was to 'talk their own words' on the Sabbath? We know how embarrassing it can be when someone injects into a serious discussion an insensitive, trivial remark which is right off the point. To be talking our own words in the context of the Sabbath is infinitely worse. God's intention in giving the people the Sabbath was that they might irreproachably be preoccupied with him, to worship him and learn from him. The love of which we have been speaking lies at the heart of our relationship with him, and we are in a sorry condition if we find ourselves short of matter with which to occupy our thoughts and our tongues in this area! There really ought to be a spontaneity of expression—*declaring* God's love and faithfulness. It must be said, though, that it is something which needs to be encouraged and developed. It was observed that the worship of God was activity which was intended to occupy the whole of the day. During the day there would have been occasions for formal meeting. Outside of these times the people of God would have spent time together, over meals and in conversation for example. It is not so different in the Christian church. If on the Lord's day we meet twice as a local church, there is the remainder of the day to be occupied. Perhaps many churches would do well to give some thought to how their members could spend more time together in fellowship in more intimate groups. It is not so difficult to talk together of things we have learnt from God's Word, and surely there are many ways in which we can testify to God's faithfulness toward us in our own experience? Then there may be ways in which we can speak of his love and faithfulness to others who are still in the dark, by visiting or by using opportunities which present themselves in our particular circumstances. If we wish to, there is no shortage of ways in which we can use a day in which our conversation revolves around the Lord our God, his Word and his works, and in particular his dealings with us and others.

The answers to these three questions raised in the course of Isaiah's call for true Sabbath observance should have made it plain to us that God's intention was to draw his people close to him, bringing them into the kind of fellowship where they could enjoy and find security in his love, and hence be useful in his service.

Those who view the Sabbath in terms of its being a blessing, wholeheartedly welcome the opportunities it provides to worship and serve God. For them the day is as short as for the others it is long.

Three classes of people

We now turn to another passage in Isaiah's prophecy. Please read Isaiah 56:1-8. It would appear this passage addresses three classes of people. The first class probably comprises Israelites who had a natural right of access to the temple and 'the assembly of the Lord', the second those who were not Israelites by birth, and the third who were excluded on account of their being eunuchs (Deuteronomy 23:1). Following on from that amazingly detailed prophecy in chapters 52 and 53 about the humiliation, suffering and exaltation of the 'Servant' of the Lord, Isaiah enlarges on the wonderful blessings which accompany the proclamation of the gospel message; blessings which, as he has indicated on so many occasions already, are not to be restricted to the Israelites alone but are to extend to all nations. So in chapter 56 he addresses both those who thought they had some right of access to these blessings and those who either believed they were, or feared they might be, excluded from them. In the one case God tells them not to 'presume because...', while in the other he tells them not to 'assume because...'. Presumption and assumption must both be forsaken as having no rightful place when we encounter the God of grace!

To Israelites who presumed some right to God's blessing he reminds them that there was nothing hereditary or automatic about it. The man who would be blessed (verse 2) was the man who laid hold on justice and righteousness, and you can't lay hold on these things and hang on to evil practices at the same time! The one has to be released in order to grasp the other. This makes good sense. But why the mention of the Sabbath?

In order to answer this I must make some observations on the structure of the poetic style of the Hebrew here. In each clause there are parallels. Thus in verse 1 both *justice* and *righteousness* are mentioned, the one to be *kept*, the other to be *done*. Keeping the same theme in mind, in verse 1b we read of *salvation* and *righteousness*, the one which is about to *come*, the other about to be *revealed*. In verse 2 there is the promise of a blessing. To whom? To *the man*, and then to *the son of man*; to the one who *does* it and to the other who *lays hold* on it. Obviously these are not two classes of people doing different things, but the second of the two clauses emphasises the first. I said this was probably intended primarily for the Israelites who considered themselves to be 'in on' the promises of God. The Lord emphasises that the blessing is to the *man* (or woman!) who does certain things. This matter concerns humanity in general, and therefore the Israelite in particular, not because he is an Israelite but because he is a member of humanity, and especially because as an Israelite he has been enormously privileged to know the truth, a privilege which carries with it great responsibilities. Then in the second part of verse 2 we again have parallelism, the first clause concerning the honouring of the Sabbath, and the second concerning right conduct, both here being cast in negative form as appropriate to the class of people to whom this is addressed. More than that, though, it rounds off the paragraph, which commenced with the maintenance of justice and righteousness and now concludes with abstinence from conduct which would undermine them. Thus Isaiah, writing under the inspiration of the Holy Spirit, sees true Sabbath observance hand in glove with the maintenance of the whole of the law of commandments.

Next, continuing the grand theme he has begun, the prophet turns to those of foreign extraction (verse 3), regarded and treated as such by the Israelites and excluded from the privileges pertaining to the worship at the temple. Although not all translations of the Bible make it clear, a figure of speech is used here. In verse 2 there was mention of 'the son of man', while here we read of 'the son of the foreigner'. This expression is a device to emphasise the fact that this person is not simply a foreigner, but *very much* a foreigner. He is not looking at a door which is ajar into which he might cautiously place his foot. Far from it. The door is barred and bolted, the outer gate is shut with all manner of security against entrance, and he is on the outside of that. He is 'utterly separated', or 'excluded'. He cannot in his wildest dreams hope to have a place with the people of God. The typical attitude of the Jews was that he was on the outside looking in, and must ever remain there. Foreigner though he might be, he is nevertheless envisaged by Isaiah as 'joining himself to the Lord'.

Before he says anything further about the foreigner, Isaiah next turns to the plight of the eunuch who similarly, though in this case among the people of God, was excluded from the temple, even if he chose to please God and had embraced his covenant.

So what does God say to these two classes of people? He says they are not to assume that the Lord has separated them from his people as having no place, and no hope of a place, with them (verse 3). The eunuch was not to assume that his condition or situation in life automatically banned him from the Lord's blessing. Here are two groups of people, both with serious natural deficiencies and disadvantages which they thought would certainly debar them from any interest in the benefits God was to bestow upon his people.

This is nothing new. How many people find reason to suppose they are, for some reason in themselves, excluded from the spiritual blessings others are entitled to? They long for God, they desire earnestly to live for him, but they groan inwardly because of what they are, or what they have done, assuming they are thereby excluded from, or have excluded themselves from, what others may legitimately enjoy. Maybe some reader finds himself or herself in this position at this very moment. Your heart aches because you assume that something about your past stands between you and God, between you and his people, so that he will (rightly, you say) never be to you what he is to others. If that is the case, there is a surprise for you in these verses. Not only is there a rebuke—'Don't say such a thing of God' (verse 3)—but there is a promise of unimaginable blessings. The eunuch, as just observed, was excluded from the temple, even if he chose to please God and embraced his covenant. What did God promise him? A place in his house and within his walls (verse 5). That was unimaginable. Then the eunuch was at the end of the family line, his name soon to be forgotten, dying out with him. That was inevitable. What did God promise him? A name better than sons and daughters, an *everlasting* name that would not be cut off. That was inconceivable (excuse the pun)! You see how God loves to magnify his grace in the face of the impossible? People might have said of the eunuch, 'His name will perish with him.' How far wide of the mark they would have been! Now if God could do that for the eunuch, what might he do for you? Do not assume. What you are is no obstacle to God, and what you have done is no obstacle to him, either. What you are, what you have done, provide an opportunity for him to display the riches of his grace toward you in Christ.

And what about the foreigner who suffered under the stigma of not really belonging (verse 3), even though he committed himself to following the Lord (verse 6)? God speaks of bringing him to his holy mountain (verse 7); that is, bringing him, with others, to the place of his presence; of making him joyful in his house of prayer because it is to be called a house of prayer *for all nations*. He *brings* such people (verse 7), he *gathers* them (verse 8), and he demonstrates to them that this is where they *belong*. It is for *them* just as much as it is for others. In fact, the distinction between 'them' and 'others' is itself rendered void. If you love the Lord and his Word and yet have any reason to think that you don't properly belong among God's people, you will have a hard time proving it in the light of what God says here!

So why the mention of the Sabbath in each case? No. That is the wrong way of putting it. Why is the Sabbath the central feature concerning all three categories of people? Here is an Israelite, and he is keeping the Sabbath day holy (as might be expected, we say). But here is a eunuch, and in spite of his disadvantages, he too is keeping the Sabbath and choosing what pleases God. Furthermore, here too is a foreigner, and without regard to what his fellow-countrymen do, he is keeping the Sabbath as well and holding fast to the covenant God gave his people. What does this demonstrate? It surely demonstrates that keeping the Sabbath—in the sense that God intended it should be kept—lies at the heart of the covenant relationship of God with his people: not for his people Israel only, but for all the Gentiles who were called by his name (Amos 9:12, quoted in Acts 15:17). The Sabbath, as Jesus later said (and as we shall consider in more detail later) was not made simply for the Jews, but for man.

It is worth mentioning at this point that the apostle Paul takes up this theme of exclusion in his letter to the Ephesians, referring to the plight of the Gentiles in their total ignorance of the truth and its inaccessibility (2:12). This is the 'middle wall of separation' of 2:14. Lest someone misunderstands what he means when he writes of 'abolishing ... the law of commandments' and concludes that he is saying the commandments are no longer relevant, let us be clear about what he is saying in context. The Jews had had the law of commandments as their constitutional document (as we observed before). What Jesus abolished was not the commandments themselves. Paul recognizes this quite clearly because, as we read on in this same letter, in chapters 4 and 5 he urges upon his readers conduct which unmistakably conforms to the Ten Commandments. More than that, at 6:2 he actually quotes the Fifth Commandment in such a way as upholds its validity. Remember that in chapter 2 Paul is addressing Gentiles who would have been very conscious of their separation from the Jews and the religion of the Jews (Ephesians 2:11-12). To them the Jews' law towered between them like a mighty barrier, the 'middle wall of separation'. If the basis of acceptance was in this law, they most certainly were excluded. But, says the apostle, the basis of acceptance is not in this law, but in what Jesus Christ has accomplished in his flesh. He, not the law, is the source of acceptance with God for both Jew and Gentile, and *in this respect* the law is abolished. It no longer presents an insurmountable obstacle, for Jew and Gentile are united in Christ through faith and new birth (Ephesians 2:8,5,15b-16).

Jeremiah, a thorn in the side

Jeremiah prophesied at perhaps the darkest point in the history of the nation of Israel. Idolatry was rampant; political manoeuvring instead of seeking God was the method used to promote the national interest and security; godliness was looked upon with suspicion and contempt; corruption, greed, exploitation and treachery were undermining the very fabric of society. Yet in spite of all this degradation there were people proclaiming a message of hope and peace and they were being listened to. Having exchanged the truth of God for a lie (Romans 1:25) they were given over to a judicial blindness which prevented them from seeing what was staring them in the face. Virtually nobody from any part of that society feared God. It was to such a people that Jeremiah found himself preaching, and he used every method in the book to seek to win people back to the truth and to trust in the LORD. He had to address people who did not want to hear him, to whom he was a thorn in their side. Under divine compulsion he pointed out the people's sins, pleading with them as he yearned for their repentance and restoration.

As well as addressing these issues which were like cancer leading them inexorably toward their death throes, Jeremiah was called upon to undertake a tour of the city gates, preaching in each on the need for Sabbath observance (17:19-27). On any day of the week there would through these gates be incessant comings and goings of people carrying on their business, which invariably involved their bearing burdens of all kinds, whether on foot or using camels or carts. So what did Jeremiah say? He told them quite simply that this had to stop (verse 21). Even at that time, we can be sure the people knew the law concerning the Sabbath. But to them it evidently did not matter. Life had to go on, and to them there was no time for artificial breaks. As well as the need for this disobedience to stop, Jeremiah adds the requirement to 'hallow the Sabbath day' as God had commanded centuries before (verse 22). I suppose people might have remonstrated with Jeremiah that the Sabbath had never been strictly observed and that now was hardly the time to start. They would have been wrong, of course, but what is recorded as having been done in the dim and distant past seems to lack relevance for the present. 'That was then, but this is now.' This in itself is an age-old argument in which pragmatism usurps principle. Jeremiah uses an 'if...then' argument (verses 24-25) reminiscent of Isaiah's already considered, in which God appends promises to the fulfilling of the conditions he imposes (see also Jeremiah 22:4). But again, the riches of the promise would have been lost on the mercenary minded, to whom the bringing of sacrifices of praise into the house of the Lord would have meant little or nothing.

What are we to conclude from Jeremiah's preaching concerning the Sabbath? Firstly, we are reminded that the Sabbath was so important to God that its continued neglect would result in destruction for the people called by his name (verse 27). Secondly, the call to Sabbath observance proved to be a test of the people's willingness to take God seriously. God was telling the people that they were doing wrong. What he wanted from them was an acknowledgement that this was so, supported by practical steps to remedy the fault. Where self-interest and God's commands come into conflict, God requires us first to acknowledge we are wrong and he is right, and then to take action in keeping with our confession. Repentance without reformation may be called by its real name: hypocrisy. John the Baptist did not mince his words in this respect (Matthew 3:7-12). For, thirdly, true repentance finds a God who is true to his word, providing the will and power for reformation, leading on into the appreciation of the blessings of which he speaks.

We may note that God appends the promises of verses 25-26 upon one aspect of obedience only: hallowing the Sabbath. When we compare 22:1-4 we find essentially the same promise appended to the different conditions of obedience stated in verse 3: 'Execute judgement and righteousness and deliver the plundered out of the hand of the oppressor. Do no wrong and do no violence to the stranger, the fatherless, or the widow, nor shed innocent blood in this place.' This is yet another proof that hallowing the Sabbath and maintaining justice and righteousness with compassion are inseparable companions. If the people had had a mind to do one, they would also have done the other.

There is the very real danger that some reading this book will be doing so with closed minds. You have already made up your mind about the Sabbath, that it is a thing of the past. Therefore God cannot be calling you to take any reformative action in respect of the Fourth Commandment. Furthermore, you are getting on quite well enough as you are and can see no need to take any personal action which will bring you more into line with it. You have seen from what has been thus far considered on the subject that it is much more far-reaching than you originally supposed, but pragmatism weighs more heavily than principle. My plea, in the dark days in which we are living, is that you ponder with the utmost seriousness the words of the living God, seeking his obedience whatever the personal cost to yourself. Jeremiah's hearers forfeited everything through failing to take God's word seriously. They thought all was well, but they had dramatically deceived themselves.

Ezekiel the watchman

In about 597 BC, at the end of the second invasion of Judah by Nebuchadnezzar, king of Babylon, Jehoiachin, king of Judah, was taken into exile with ten thousand other captives (2 Kings 24:11-16), among whom was Ezekiel. Eight years before that, in 605 BC, Daniel had been among the Jewish captives of the first deportation (Daniel 1:1-3). Thus at that period there were three great contemporary prophets: Jeremiah, prophet mainly to the Jews in Jerusalem, before the city fell; Daniel, prophet mainly to the royal court and administration in Babylon and later to the Persians; Ezekiel, prophet mainly to the Jewish exiles in Babylon.

Our attention will be directed toward Ezekiel, and the 20th chapter of the book bearing his name. Among the Jewish community 'by the river Chebar' in Babylonia, exiled from their homeland, Ezekiel had been established as a prophet (1:3). From time to time the elders of the people came to Ezekiel (compare 20:1 with 8:1 and 14:1). It is clear they were being given a hard time by the prophet, and yet they kept coming.

Ezekiel's ministry to them was an interesting one. Systematically, through his servant, God was dismantling their false expectation and hope for their nation, their self complacency with lives which failed to conform to God's standards, and the idea that they had any ability to retrieve the situation. The elders, as leaders among the people, were being made to see the stubbornness of unbelief, and the reluctance of the human heart to lay aside cherished fancies, that they might be brought to the conclusion that apart from God's grace alone their situation was utterly hopeless. As in the previous case (14:1), the precise reason for their coming to Ezekiel on this occasion is not given. Maybe they wanted enlightenment concerning their perplexing circumstances, maybe some direction for the future, but God looked into their hearts and bypassed what they *thought* they wanted from him to put his finger on their real need (verses 3, 31). There were clearly certain things they had yet to understand about God and about themselves.

Five times (verses 5, 6, 15, 23, 28) God is described as 'raising his hand' in confirmation of his promises. Put in human terms, he is putting himself under oath to perform what he has said. The unstated question being put to the elders was this: 'Did God do what he promised?' They knew the answer, of course, that God did keep his promises. At first sight verses 6 and 15 are contradictory: God promised he would do something, and then he promised he would not do that self-same thing! What are we to make of it? We must note carefully the application of an important principle here. First, God fulfils his promises of blessing, and the faithful enter into it; second, to those who by unbelief spurn his blessings he promises judgement, and the faithless fall under it. In this connection read Romans 11:22 and see also Numbers 14:26-30. Thus there is no contradiction. As the writer to the Hebrews says in a passage we shall consider later: 'So we see that they could not enter in because of unbelief' (Hebrew 3:19).

Then three times (verses 9, 14, 22) we read of God acting for his own honour, described as 'for my name's sake'; and you will observe that each time he is concerned for his honour in the eyes of the Gentiles. Why should God care what the Gentiles think? The answer is simple: it is that the Gentiles might hope in him (Romans 15:8-13). This had always been in God's heart throughout the history of the nation of Israel. There are two strands to why God was so concerned. The first is that the Gentiles should understand that here is a God who speaks and acts; the second is that here is a God who is glorious in majesty, whose name will be exalted throughout the earth. As Christians we need to retain these two strands in our thinking in relation to God's dealings with us. Non-Christians around us observe us and, though they may say little, in us they witness God's faithfulness to his promises and the honour of his name.

If you have read the chapter, you will know that the Sabbath features prominently in Ezekiel's message to these leaders of the Jews. In particular, in verses 12 and 20 he quotes Exodus 31:13, and it confirms what we said earlier about their observance of the Sabbath as being a sign to the Gentile nations round about. The Sabbath was intended by God as a special privilege and honour among his people for the enjoyment and deepening of the covenant relationship. It was to be carefully guarded against all unwarranted intrusions. As such, it was a powerful witness among the surrounding nations to whom such a notion was entirely foreign. Its abuse was so serious because it struck at the heart of the covenant relationship; hence its mention in verses 13, 16, 21, 24.

Will you note especially that Ezekiel draws a direct line connecting the people's rebellion against God (verse 8) with their defiling the Sabbath (verse 16). Their failure to keep the Sabbath holy as commanded (verse 20) was a mark of their refusal to listen to God (verse 8). Their profaning of the Sabbath went hand in hand with their despising of God's statutes and not honouring what he judged to be right (verse 24).

What Ezekiel sees here has nothing whatever to do with the people's failure in respect of a ceremonial matter or a legalistic requirement. He lays it on the line: their hearts were still in the world; at heart they were still just like their forefathers. Hence the reference to the idols of Egypt (verse 8), and their subsequent idolatry in the land of Canaan (verses 18, 31). The supreme, overriding evidence that their hearts were in the world, lay in their attitude to the Sabbath, because they refused publicly to acknowledge the sign God had given them that they were exclusively to belong to him (verse 12), in keeping with his declaration, 'I am the LORD your God' (verse 5).

This is why, each time there is mention of the people's failure in regard to the statutes and judgements God had given them, the profaning of the Sabbath features in the repetitive cycle. However, it does not merely feature, it is given a dramatic prominence. In verses 16 and 21, though the prophet repeats that God had given them statutes by which to live and they had failed to keep them, the comparison is now not between their receiving his statutes and not keeping *them*, but between their receiving his statutes and not keeping the *Sabbath*. The point of contention is not, 'I gave you my laws but you broke them' (true though that was), but, 'I gave you my laws but you treated the Sabbath with contempt.' What he says directly and unequivocally is this: God had given them statutes and judgements by which they might live, 'but they profaned *my Sabbaths.*' What was the public face to their disregard for what God had commanded? It was their conduct on the Sabbath. The Sabbath is at the very centre of the prophet's judgement upon the people (verse 4). What happened in the daily life of the individual, of the family, of the nation, revolved around what happened on the Sabbath. The indicator of the spiritual health of the nation was in their attitude to the Sabbath. What they thought and did on the Sabbath day determined whether in their hearts they wanted to be like everybody else (verse 32) or whether they wanted to be God's sanctified people (verse 12). If they weren't Sabbath-keepers, they were idolaters (verses 16, 24); if they weren't idolaters, they would hallow the Sabbath. Did they want God, or did they want only the benefits this world had to offer? Look at their conduct on the Sabbath, and you have your answer.

I will be so bold at this point to suggest that nothing has changed. The professing Christian's attitude toward the Fourth Commandment still provides a litmus test of his or her heart for God. There is dreadful confusion today about this matter, and it all reduces to one simple factor: the church has lost touch with the God of the covenant, has failed in respect of the separation that belonging to Christ demands (yes, demands, for Christ's commands are to be obeyed—2 Corinthians 6:17). The professing church has flirted with the world, the attitudes of the world, the standards of the world, the enticements of the world, the philosophies of the world, until by and large the distinctions have become so blurred that black and white have been reduced to various shades of grey. The professing church has lost confidence in the only thing which it needs, the enduring and unchanging and unfailingly dependable word of the God who cannot lie. The church abuses the grace of God by throwing the law back in his face and acting as if it has no relevance now, thus degrading the accomplishment of Christ upon the cross of Calvary and cheapening the unspeakable glory of his finished work. The reader who is offended by these remarks may readily identify himself or herself with how the elders of Israel felt who heard exactly the same thing from the prophet Ezekiel. Our greatest need is for true, deep repentance for our neglect of the whole counsel of God in favour of other things of no consequence by comparison, and to give ourselves, heart, mind, soul and strength, to his Word.

Nehemiah the reformer

Finally, we turn back in our Bibles, but on in time, to Nehemiah. There are indications that Ezekiel's message eventually got through and that many people were prepared by God for what happened among the exiles who eventually returned to Jerusalem and Judah. In the book of Nehemiah we discover some further interesting things about the Sabbath, the first of which is in chapter 9, verse 14.

The scene before us is an extraordinary one, a huge gathering of people deeply affected by the word of God, their hearts having been smitten by their disobedience, moving them to tears of repentance and then again to the heights of joy because they had understood God's word and knew now something of what it meant to be under his blessing. But repentance leads to reformation. So they had solemnly gathered to confess God's goodness, likewise to confess their badness, and set on record their promise to obey him. At some point the Levites stood to lead in public prayer—clearly carefully prepared in advance—to bless the Lord and acknowledge what he had done in calling out a people to himself. When they came to the giving of the law (verses 13-14) they stated appreciatively that God had given them *good* statutes and commandments as well as *just* ordinances and *true* laws. The law, they acknowledged, was absolutely beneficial to them, and they were profoundly thankful for it. It is characteristic of people whose hearts are touched by the grace of God, that they greatly value his commandments. As they said this, the Levites singled out the Sabbath, giving it special mention, using a very interesting expression: 'You *made known* to them your holy Sabbath.' Among the commandments which were *given*, the Sabbath was *made known*. The implication in this statement is twofold. Firstly, it confirms that it had already existed. The Sabbath was not something which was made for the occasion of the inauguration of the nation of Israel. More than that, though, it would seem that its being 'made known' indicated a considerable measure of former ignorance about it. Quite probably the people, though acquainted with the existence of the weekly cycle, had never really grasped the *meaning* behind it. The time had come for God to dispel their ignorance and make known to them what it was all about. This was God's holy Sabbath, a week by week reminder that all of creation was his, to worship and honour him. This was the time to put to one side the day to day routines of life in order to give undivided attention to God, a time also to learn from him and to be equipped for living in his world with reference to him.

It is not without significance that the leaders should highlight the Sabbath in this way at a time of spiritual revival among the people. When the Spirit of God moves among his people with the result of bringing the realities of life and eternity into clearer focus, the first thing to be treasured is our relationship with him, and the first thing jealously to be guarded is time that we might spend in his presence.

The reference to the Sabbath in Nehemiah 9:14 embeds it firmly and centrally in the law. It isn't separate or a stand-alone entity. Nor is it a vestigial organ to be excised from the law now that we have grown into maturity! However, this singling out of the Sabbath, and the way it is described, does seem to give it a special place as being larger than the law, even though a part of it. The Levites were declaring they had been blessed with this special revelation. Not surprisingly therefore, the reformation they promised to undertake by solemn covenant (9:38—10:39) included practical steps to guard the Sabbath from unwanted intrusions (10:31).

As is common knowledge, it is one thing to make a promise, it is another to keep it. What is fine in theory sometimes presents awkward difficulties in practice. What is maintained in the fervour of enthusiasm can fall into disuse when zeal abates. It seems to be a general principle that sooner or later promises are put to the test. Nehemiah the governor was away back in Persia for some years after this (13:6), and when he returned again to Jerusalem a sorry picture presented itself to his view. Comparing the promise of 10:31 with the practice of 13:15-16 we may be astonished that some of the very people who had appended their names to the covenant were now completely disregarding it. It could not have been just a few, either, because the merchants clearly considered it worth their while to do business on the Sabbath.

But should we be astonished? Do we not see the same thing all around us, and even in our churches? Dare we ask whether we see it also in our personal lives? Spiritual laxity seems to be the order of the day. Where there is clear-cut and uncompromising faithfulness to the Word of God it is often interpreted as narrow-minded legalism; where one dares to utter a rebuke to 'easy-going' Christianity he or she does so at the risk of being accused of a censorious spirit. We can be sure Nehemiah was far from popular when he warned the people about trading on the Sabbath, when he reasoned with and rebuked the nobility, a class who seldom take kindly to this sort of treatment, and when he tackled the traders themselves and put the lid on their trading on the Sabbath.

It is at such times of spiritual laxity that 'enthusiasm' can be a word endued with negative connotations. It is all very well, one might say, but we've got to live in the real world, the inference being that what was done in the time of 'enthusiasm' was living in a make-believe world. Nothing could be further from the truth where spiritual revival is concerned. What had been experienced before Nehemiah returned to Persia was a taste of reality, with God, and their enjoyment of God, the hub around which the whole of their lives began to revolve. Sadly, it did not last all that long, so that many in the generation following had lost contact with this vital truth. In many ways, it is sad that Nehemiah had to act as he did upon his second return to Jerusalem (13:4-31), because, although he was right to take action, it reflected upon a state of affairs which could not really be remedied by the imposition of sanctions. The only real hope was that what he did would sober the people into a recall and recognition of the height from which they had fallen, renewing them to repentance and a return to their first love.

In the light of what is recorded in Nehemiah 13, perhaps a word of caution is in order for ourselves when faced with contentious issues, that neither should we handle them in a contentious fashion, nor should we take the law into our own hands. Nehemiah was careful to explain his grave concerns as he gave his rebuke (verses 17-18). However, as governor he had a responsibility not only to warn, but also to act. He did so incisively, but not unreasonably, by ordering the gates to be shut during the Sabbath, and his threat of laying hands on the traders, real and valid though it was, did not have to be put to the test (verse 21). Within the local church issues may arise which call for action, but while we all have responsibility to exhort one another to holy living (Hebrews 3:13), disciplinary action when it is needed is the responsibility of the God-appointed leaders.

To conclude, the prophets spoke with one voice in declaring that keeping the Sabbath was the moral responsibility of the people. It had nothing to do with ceremony or typology, but everything to do with their relationship with God. When their relationship with God was right, then they valued and guarded the Sabbath; when they neglected, despised or abused the Sabbath, it proved their relationship with God was all wrong. The health of their vertical relationship with God was reflected in the health of their horizontal relationship with their fellow men and women. The Sabbath was absolutely central to the spiritual wellbeing of the LORD's people, because he gave it to be so.

Chapter 6

The Lord of the Sabbath

In the preceding chapters we have built up a picture from the Old Testament of what the Sabbath was intended to be. Is this picture an accurate one? Has our interpretation been faithful? The more complete revelation of the New Testament must provide the criteria by which we answer these questions. What do Jesus and his apostles have to teach us about this matter? The New Testament is as much a part of the inspired Word of God as the Old. It is the same God who 'breathed' both (2 Timothy 3:16). He has not changed, nor has he changed his mind. His eternal counsels have found their fullest expression in 'the Word made flesh'.

So we come now to a consideration of the Sabbath in the Gospels. The Lord Jesus Christ kept the Sabbath perfectly, as he kept the whole of the law perfectly. The law, which was holy and just and good (Romans 7:12) and which exposed the apostle Paul as being otherwise, found its exemplar in Jesus, who was holy and just and good. If we would understand the Fourth Commandment in practice, who better to consider than Jesus himself in his use of the Sabbath? So, having seen the centrality of the Sabbath in the Old Testament in the relationship of God to his people, our attention now turns to the attitude of Jesus to the Sabbath day.

We do not have to read far into the Gospels to discover that much of the contention between Jesus and the Pharisees revolved around his use of the Sabbath day. Many regard this as merely one bone of contention between them and little more than a demonstration of the narrow-minded legalism of the Pharisees. I hope to show in these pages that it was far more than that, and that Jesus was reinstating something which the religious leaders had fettered with prohibitions and a host of rules and regulations. He makes a number of telling statements and gives a number of searching examples to show us what the Sabbath is really all about.

Two big statements

We begin with a study of the section from which our chapter heading is derived: Mark 2:23—3:6 and the parallel passage in Matthew 12:1-8.

(Luke also mentions the incident—6:1-5.) For all its simplicity, there has been much confusion over the statement Jesus made when he said: 'The Sabbath was made for man and not man for the Sabbath' (Mark 2:27), and its sequel: 'Therefore the Son of Man is also Lord of the Sabbath.' If we would be clear about the meaning we need to appreciate what led up to this statement, which is an accusation by the Pharisees that Jesus' disciples were breaking the Sabbath by plucking heads of grain and eating them as they went through the fields.

The religious leaders evidently had Jesus under close observation from a very early point in his public ministry. Not being of their school, he was regarded with suspicion, and the nature of their questions thinly veils a deep-rooted and growing hostility. The Pharisees were very particular about the observance of the Law, expanding it into a great number of detailed rules and regulations so that, in their estimation, it might properly be followed. Jesus' manner of dealing with the accusation at hand is very telling.

As an aside, it is noteworthy that the Pharisees could find so little to pick up on by way of accusing Jesus and his disciples of Sabbath breaking, when clearly they were trying so very hard to find fault! This only serves to underline that Jesus was as careful (if that is the right word) in respect of keeping the Sabbath as he was in keeping the whole of the law. Apart from this incident in the fields, it would seem that the only other area in which he was accused of 'breaking' the Sabbath was in his healing people on that day.

A technical point?

The first observation to make is that in plucking the heads of grain and eating, the disciples were certainly doing something which was lawful in itself because, interestingly, the law specifically mentions this very thing, for Deuteronomy 23:24-25 says, 'When you come into your neighbour's vineyard, you may eat your fill of grapes at your pleasure, but you shall not put any in your container. When you come into your neighbour's standing grain, you may pluck the heads with your hand, but you shall not use a sickle on your neighbour's standing grain.' The Pharisees would have been well aware of this. But, because they were zealous in their strict interpretation of the law of Moses (which, by the way, was far from being a bad thing in and of itself), plucking grain and removing the husks they considered equivalent to threshing, which was work, and so was forbidden on the Sabbath. Therefore, according to their interpretation, although *what* the disciples were doing was lawful, *when* they were doing it was not.

We need at this point to note that the difference between the Pharisees and Jesus on the subject of the use of the Sabbath was one of *interpretation* of the law, not the *words* of the law. There was no dispute over what the Law said, only over what it meant. This is precisely the problem today. We may know what the law says, but how are we to interpret and therefore apply it?

The motive which lay behind the Pharisees' accusation, had we not previously been aware of it, comes out into the open later, for they were really looking for a reason to accuse Jesus (Mark 3:2). This confuses the picture, because at the bottom of the dispute there is more going on than an objective concern for truth. Regrettably this is very often the case, because prejudice and preconceived notions often colour our attitudes. However, we must not mix up people's practices with their motives and, as the saying goes, throw out the baby with the bath water.

If we had been caught unawares with the question, 'Why do they do what is not lawful on the Sabbath?', we might have responded by looking at the issue of what the disciples were doing and the Pharisees' interpretation of it—leaving aside their motivation for the moment— and argued about where the line was to be drawn between what was legitimate and what was not on the Sabbath. Another issue of the same kind is embodied in what was called a 'Sabbath day's journey' (Acts 1:12—which is interesting in that this well-understood term was based upon tradition and not upon the law). How many miles were they permitted to walk on the Sabbath without breaking it? At what point was the division to be made between what was lawful and what was not? Instances could be multiplied of situations in which we ask the question: 'Just where do we draw the line?' The question may be a valid one, but it raises another: By what *criteria* are we to decide where the line is to be drawn? If there are no criteria, then we have to conclude that either the question is not valid or that it becomes a matter of opinion—and people are entitled to their opinions without others coming along and imposing theirs upon them!

For many Christians who uphold the Sabbath principle the problem arises not simply as to what should or should not be done on the Sabbath or the Lord's Day, but *how to decide* what should or should not be done. For the non-Sabbatarian there is no problem: the question is irrelevant. But for those who believe the Fourth Commandment should be observed, they do need to be clear about what the criteria are. For example, is it permissible for Christians to use public transport on a Sunday? Does it make any difference if they are doing so to go to a church meeting? Or what about Christians whose job involves Sunday work from time to time? What should they do about it? Is it *wrong* for them to work on the day? Are they breaking God's law? Does it depend, perhaps, on what the work is? Or, should you do anything on a Sunday which involves *others* working—like posting letters, or eating out, or staying in a hotel? Does it depend upon the circumstances? What is a 'Sabbath Day's journey' today—by car? Is the sale of Christian books from a church bookstall permissible on a Sunday? These, and similar examples, show what a minefield we can be entering when we begin to think about such things. Indeed, Christians have divided sharply over just such issues as these.

For these reasons it is important that we learn from the way Jesus tackled the problem. He did not debate it; nor did he side-step it. He did not look at the issue in the way we might so easily have done. What he did was to tackle the *real* issue. The matter of picking ears of wheat on the Sabbath was only the smoke screen.

When Jesus said in Mark 2:28, 'Therefore the Son of Man is also Lord of the Sabbath,' what did he mean? On the surface of it he appears to have been justifying his disciples' actions in his answer to the Pharisees by taking Old Testament examples of people who had done what was *not* lawful on the Sabbath—and people have said as much! We're not to follow the law any longer, they say, but we are to follow Jesus. According to them, the law is defective, because it is shown by Jesus at this point to be so when he justifies David in breaking it (verse 26). Others say that Jesus was reinterpreting the Sabbath law, in much the same way as, they argue, he reinterpreted the laws about adultery and murder in Matthew 5.

We ought therefore to examine the two cases cited in connection with the Sabbath, one in Mark 2:25-26 and the other in Matthew 12:5.

Did the priests desecrate the Sabbath?

To take the Matthew passage first, Jesus refers to the priests in the temple 'profaning' or 'desecrating' the Sabbath and being blameless. It is a strong word to use, 'profane', or 'desecrate'. So what exactly were they doing? At Numbers 28:9-10 we read: '*On the Sabbath day* [offer] two lambs in their first year, without blemish, and two-tenths of an ephah of fine flour as a grain offering, mixed with oil, with its drink offering—this is the burnt offering for every Sabbath, besides the regular burnt offering with its drink offering.' The point (which the Pharisees would have understood) is that this is the very thing the priests had been doing all week. It was their work to which they had been called. The preceding verses in Numbers refer to the *daily* offering. In fact, far from resting, it seems they were required to do *more* work on the Sabbath! (Their service on the Sabbath, whether or not they recognized it, was in its symbolism pointing emphatically to Christ's saving work and therefore indicating that the Sabbath had special significance in God's redemptive purposes.)

Now, says Jesus to these legalistic Pharisees, while you accept without question the legitimacy of the priests' actions on the Sabbath, according to the very same principle which you apply in other areas you are really saying that the priests are *profaning* the Sabbath. You can't have it both ways!

Jesus is using the Pharisees' own logic against themselves. According to their own standards, they must have it that the priests are profaning the Sabbath. Of course, the priests are not desecrating what is holy, for otherwise they would not be blameless. So it is not *Jesus* who is saying they are profaning the Sabbath, but the *Pharisees*, and Jesus is simply putting the words into their mouths because that is where their own logic leads them. The priests are indeed blameless, says Jesus, They are acting honourably, because on the Sabbath, by what they are doing, they are underlining the importance of substitutionary sacrifice. The Pharisees are acting dishonourably because in their thinking mercy and sacrifice are two entirely different things and they haven't understood either (verse 7).

Dickens, in his book *Our Mutual Friend*, describes a conversation between a certain Mr Venus and one Mr Boffin dubbed as 'The Golden Dustman' on account of the work which brought him into his fortune. Venus has just made a somewhat delicate proposition to him which requires a measure of confidentiality.

'That sounds fair,' said Mr Boffin. 'I agree to that.'

"I have your word and honour, sir?'

'My good fellow,' retorted Mr Boffin, 'you have my word; and how you can have that, without my honour too, I don't know. I've sorted a lot of dust in my time, but I never knew the two things go into separate heaps.'

This remark seemed rather to abash Mr Venus. He hesitated, and said, 'Very true, sir;' and again, 'Very true, sir,' before resuming the thread of his discourse.'

The Pharisees did not for a moment hesitate, neither were they in the least abashed, that they were putting the administration of the law and the ministry of mercy into two separate heaps as if one had nothing to do with the other. They never thought about the significance of the law on the tablets of stone being beneath the atonement cover (rather appropriately described as the mercy seat in the Authorized Version), to which the blood of sacrifice gave the only means of access, or about this being the place where God himself met with his people through forgiveness of sins. To them it was all theory, being self-centred rather than God-centred in their thinking. They had never put two and two together to think of the law as an instrument of blessing to the people and to use it accordingly.

How the Pharisees loved the temple, and the ritual, and the law, and everything associated with the temple—only they had left out of their thinking what mattered most—a living relationship with the living God! Jesus, having just spoken of the conduct of the priests in the temple (verse 5), now refers to himself as being greater, not than the priests whose conduct is under scrutiny here, but than the temple itself (verse 6). This can mean but one thing. The temple, as just observed, was the place of the ark of the covenant and symbolic of the place where God met with his people. To say that he was greater than the temple could mean only that he was God in the flesh. Had they recognized the Lord their God in all they did and honoured him, they would have recognized also the One he sent into the world and honoured him, too (John 3:17; 5:23; 10:36).

Did the priests waive the law?

The other matter we must take up (in Mark 2:26) is that of the priest Ahimelech (Abiathar was his son—1 Samuel 22:20) giving the showbread to David and his men—on the Sabbath day at that. We can read of what happened in 1 Samuel 21:1-6, when David was fleeing for his life from the murderous intent of jealous Saul. As it happened there was no other bread available, so that the alternative to giving him the showbread was to let him and his men go away hungry, when they were clearly portrayed as being in need. Leviticus 24:5-9 gives the regulations concerning the showbread, concluding that 'it shall be for Aaron and his sons, and they shall eat it in a holy place; for it is most holy to him from the offerings of the Lord made by fire, by a perpetual statute.' This principle was established at Aaron's ordination, where, in Exodus 29:32-33 we read: 'Then Aaron and his sons shall eat the flesh of the ram, and the bread [that is, the showbread] that is in the basket, by the door of the tabernacle of meeting. They shall eat those things with which the atonement was made, to consecrate and to sanctify them; but an outsider shall not eat them, because they are holy.' So it appears to be quite clear, does it not, that Ahimelech should not have given the bread to David, because it was lawful only for the priests to eat it?

Why, then, did Jesus cite this case? Is he quoting a similar example of lawbreaking to justify his disciples in the present case? Those who are parents know very well the argument which goes: 'But my friend Jimmy is allowed to do it, so why can't I?' Just because Jimmy is allowed to do something doesn't make it right, and doesn't make it permissible for you to do it either. No, Jesus can hardly have been following that line of argument!

Or was it to say to the Pharisees: 'Now look, had we been doing something as outrageous as *that* (referring to what David did) it might have been wrong, but in fact all we are doing is *this*.' In other words, you make your actions look better by contrasting them with a much worse example! 'Oh well, if he did *that* and got away with it, then I suppose we can excuse you!' Again, clearly, Jesus was not saying any such thing!

Was it, then, to justify his disciples doing something forbidden by the law, making an appeal to the legitimacy of lawbreaking in certain instances? It can hardly be that, because what they were doing, as we have seen, was *not* forbidden by the law, only by the Pharisees' interpreted extension of the law (which rather undermines the argument of those who take this position). So that cannot be the reason, either, for Jesus speaking about the showbread.

Then what *was* the reason? It looks as if Jesus has just quoted those who did something which *wasn't* lawful to justify his disciples in doing something which *was* lawful. It hardly seems necessary, and it certainly doesn't appear to make sense! So what is he getting at? And why does he bring the argument to a conclusion by saying that the Sabbath was made for man and not man for the Sabbath, and that he is also Lord of the Sabbath?

It is only when we can answer these questions that we begin to appreciate the point he is making.

From which end are we looking at the law?

The answer to the questions just raised, surely, hinges upon *need* and *provision*. The Pharisees had a very negative view of the law. They, and so many who have followed who would not for a moment like to be lumped in with them, tend to view the law in terms of prohibition and not provision. When God gave his redeemed people the Ten Commandments, it was not with the intention to *deprive* them of any good, but to *provide* for all their needs to be met. This is an aspect of the law which is so often overlooked. Jesus and his disciples were hungry. We must remember they had no fixed means of provision and were dependent upon what was given them in the course of their ministry. It wasn't as if they were nibbling as a means of occupying themselves, as we might if *we* happened to be wandering through a field of ripe wheat. They were hungry, no one had provided for them, and here they found themselves walking through a field of grain from which the law permitted them to eat (Deuteronomy 23:24-25). The Pharisees therefore had no objection, presumably, to their eating the grain, only to extracting the kernel from the husk! That, according to their interpretation of the law, was doing work! So the law, as they understood it, was mocking these disciples' needs by presenting them with the food and not allowing them to stretch out their hands to take it. Yet they did not ask, 'Is there not a lie in my right hand?' (Isaiah 44:20).

This is why Jesus, in his infinite wisdom, referred them to the priest's recognition of *need* and his action in *providing* for David. Leaving aside the typological significance of the showbread, it was received from the people, placed upon the table, and subsequently eaten by the priests. In practical terms it was part of the way the priests were to be provided for with food; it was, if you like, a form of payment for their services, *and it was guarded by law.*

There is nothing like the smell of baking bread to awaken the appetite, even if you are not hungry, and you can imagine David arriving disconsolate and famished at Nob, where the showbread had recently been replaced with hot, freshly baked bread as happened every Sabbath, and asking for five loaves, only to be met with: 'Sorry, friend. Smells good, doesn't it? But the law says the bread is ours, so you can't have any, and as we haven't got anything else, you'll just have to go hungry.'

Ahimelech was not like the Pharisees. Shortly before he was martyred he demonstrated a true understanding of the law by giving what was rightfully his to those more needy than himself, having first sought to establish that the need was genuine and the recipients worthy. This particular law was put in place not to prevent the priests from giving what was theirs to others in case of need, but to forbid others from taking what was not theirs and thereby depriving those for whose welfare it was given. Ahimelech, therefore, was not breaking the law after all! Jesus, in citing this example, is showing the Pharisees that they are looking at the law from the wrong end. The law's prohibitions must be viewed through its provisions, not the other way round.

Thus we have seen concerning these two examples that, far from their undermining the Sabbath principle, they are actually reinforcing it against the abuse legalists had imposed upon it. The legalist *imposes* the Sabbath upon man in a list of 'dos and don'ts'. The *legalist* sees the issue from the standpoint of the *law*. The legalist says that man was made for the Sabbath. It is the Sabbath which is all-important, not man. Jesus has given these two examples to show this is not the case. The one concerning David and his men eating the consecrated bread which was reserved for the priests is a demonstration that the law is not the be-all and end-all of man's existence. One needs to go behind the law itself and assess the situation according to the principles upon which the law has been established.

Jesus is upholding the legitimacy of what David and his men did in the circumstances even though it appeared in this instance to run counter to the strict letter of the ceremonial law at this point. Note, however, that it did not in any way *undermine* the law. The law still stood as firmly as it had done before David's action. The priest Ahimelech had the wisdom to see that giving his and the priests' portion to David and his men on this occasion was necessary. Those who think the man was breaking the law could not be more badly mistaken, for he was actually *applying* it! For what he did was in reality a demonstration of the law, for it showed the law for what it was, and if anything the law gained greater respect as a result of it. The showbread was for the priests, it was part of their necessary provision, and it was guarded by this law, given to the nation as a whole, so that the priests should not be reduced to penury and be unable to continue in their vital office for lack of proper support (which in fact happened from time to time through abuse of the law). On this occasion Ahimelech exercised the prerogative of giving what was his portion by right and by statute to meet the needs of another, which was *also* a right he possessed. And thus he honoured the law because he was following the very principle enshrined in the law some said he was breaking!

In these two examples, therefore, Jesus is teaching the true purpose of the law. No bending of the law is involved whatsoever; rather, it is being upheld and displayed in its true light by these two test cases. He shows that those who are concerned merely with the letter of the law are incapable (note that word) of correctly applying it, and that the way to a true interpretation of the law is via an understanding of the spirit of the law. Jesus was therefore not undermining the law, but upholding and honouring it against those who by their narrow minded rigidity reduced it to rules and regulations as if it were an end in itself. The law is good, said Paul, if one uses it lawfully (1 Timothy 1:8). These people, though, were using it to benefit their own prestige, power and purse.

Let us gather together the main points. The first is that if we are rightly to interpret the Word of God we must come to it with the right attitude. It is insufficient to know it: we must submit to it if we are ever properly to understand it. Our own prejudices and preconceived notions, not to mention our ignorance, are often a great hindrance to understanding and applying the Scriptures, which were written for our benefit and learning. We have seen that Jesus and the Pharisees had the same law, but we know why their interpretation of it went in very different directions.

The main thing, though, to take away from the study so far, is that Jesus, far from condoning a shallow or carefree attitude to the law, and in particular the Sabbath, is actually upholding the principles enshrined in the law and demonstrating how important and valuable the law is. It should be with this ringing in our ears that we hear him declare that he is Lord of the Sabbath. He gave the Sabbath, and he gave it not that he might take it away again or change it, but rather that he might bring his people into the full enjoyment of it. This, however, is for another time.

For the present we must return to Mark 2:27-28, for we haven't yet answered the question about what Jesus meant when he said, 'The Sabbath was made for man, and not man for the Sabbath Therefore the Son of Man is also Lord of the Sabbath.' We have paved the way towards a correct interpretation of at least the first of these statements by viewing its prohibitions only in the light of its provisions. For the Pharisees the Law was an end in itself. They were its administrators, and people were to be squeezed into its straitjacket and made to walk rigidly along its narrow lines. They cared not about the people as such, only about what *they* regarded as their law, to be imposed with what *they* regarded as their God-given authority, upon those whom *they* regarded as the inferior classes! To them man was made for the Sabbath. No, says Jesus, it is the other way round. It is only when we see what the Sabbath is *for* that we understand, accept, appreciate and *welcome* its prohibitions.

When Jesus said that 'the Sabbath was made for man, and not man for the Sabbath,' note first that it was made for *man*, not simply for the Jews. True, it was *given* to the Jews, along with the other nine of the Ten Commandments, but it was not made exclusively for them, for it was *made* for man. The Jews were its custodians, as they were custodians of the law, but it did not belong or apply to them alone. Jesus quite clearly here indicates that the provisions of the Sabbath were for the benefit of mankind in general. Although he was speaking to Jews at this point, his statement does not restrict the application to them. Nor did Jesus say the Sabbath was made for *men*, but for man. It was not given to you and to me and to others to be appreciated or made use of by each individually, but it was given to us corporately, as a body, together, that *in unity together* we might have fellowship with *our* God. It is a rest in which we share together, and hence the appropriateness of our meeting together for the express purpose of together drawing near to God and of his drawing near to us.

As to how and when the Sabbath was so made, we have already observed that the Fourth Commandment itself gives us the answer in Exodus 20:11— 'For in six days the Lord made the heavens and the earth, the sea, and all that is in them, and rested the seventh day. Therefore the Lord blessed the Sabbath day and hallowed it'—and that this refers back to Genesis 2:2-3. Genesis says, 'God blessed the *seventh* day and sanctified it', while Exodus says, 'The Lord blessed the *Sabbath* day and hallowed it.'

Here a further point will be made which was only hinted at earlier. For we observe from this that the emphasis, by God's own interpretation, is not on the *seventh* day, but on the *Sabbath* day. Sabbath indicates rest, or cessation from work. It indicates that which comes at the end of what has been accomplished (a very important point to which we will return later). From God's angle at creation: 'Thus the heavens and the earth and all the host of them were finished, and on the seventh day God ended his work which he had done, and he rested on the seventh day from all his work which he had done.' From man's angle: 'Six days you shall labour and do *all* your work, but the seventh day is the Sabbath of the Lord your God.' It is very important that we understand this. There is no sanctity about the seventh day *as the seventh day*. To the question, 'Why do we not keep the seventh day of the week but the first?' the answer is partly that it was not the seventh day *per se* which God blessed, but the *Sabbath*. It was the day which indicated the cessation of work. In Old Testament times this was indeed the seventh day, based as it was upon creation. For the New Testament church Christ's saving work has introduced a new dimension into the picture. We will not digress into that now, for it will be taken up in a later chapter. For now, let us note the interpretation of God's Word and understand that the principle of the Sabbath is based upon *rest*, or *cessation*, not on the particular day of the week. Thus, as to *when* the Sabbath was made for man, the answer is: at creation. The Fourth Commandment makes this quite clear. The Sabbath was not a new concept introduced by Moses though based on creation, for then the appropriate wording would have been, 'Therefore the Lord is blessing the Sabbath day and making it holy.' On the contrary, the allusion is to something which was already in place, and the command to remember it is a re-establishment of something which may well have fallen into disuse.

As well as how and when, in an earlier chapter we considered also the question of why the Sabbath was made for man. Here I add another point. Going back to Day Six of the creation account and the creation of man, we are informed that man was created in the image of God. This means, without going into a lot of detail, that there was something about man which represented likeness to God, which distinguished him from the animals, and which enabled him to have fellowship with God. Without this, there would have been no appropriateness of God taking upon himself human flesh and appearing in the likeness of men, as he did in his Son Jesus Christ. Indeed, it would have been degrading for him and incompatible with his divine status. But such is the nature with which God invested man that he himself in the person of his Son could be clothed in the very same nature and yet retain all the dignity of his deity.

A further aspect of man's being God's image bearer is seen in his being given authority over the creation, in which he was to work and have dominion (1:26-28). Clearly this was not the work of a day, or a week, or a year, but work which would occupy him for all time. This is what some have called the 'cultural mandate'. Man was made to work. God so constituted him. Man's natural investigative inclinations into the created order are a proper expression of the way in which God has made him. His creativity was to be expressed within the framework of the creativity of God in making the heavens and the earth and all that is in them. His fruitfulness and his subjugation of every living thing to his dominion was to be an outworking of his life within the creation. What God had created was very good, but at that time it was not as he intended it ultimately to be, for he gave man a creative function within this creation.

However, God did not make man only for work, but also for rest. Man was to enter into God's rest just as much as he was to participate in work in God's creation.

Just as man's creative activity was not to be accomplished in a week, so the seventh day rest at the end of creation was intended not as a once-for-all thing, but as a weekly event. The Sabbath was a cessation, or rest, not because (as later) there was wearisome labour in his work, not because he was 'fagged out' at the end of the week and needed to put his feet up, but rather because his working was only one expression of his being, for he was made for fellowship with God. The cessation of work was not an end in itself, but it was given to serve a purpose, and that purpose was God-orientated (because the day was made holy). This was the established pattern at creation, before sin entered to mar it. Man was to work in the world in which God had placed him, and this work was not marred by anything whatsoever: it was useful, productive, enjoyable, and yet it was to be punctuated by the Sabbath rest, a special day of privileged communion with his Creator and Sustainer, in which the relationship would grow and prosper. Just as his understanding of the world would grow through his working activity, so his understanding of his God would grow through the Sabbath rest. For six days he would be devoting his mind and energy to his environment, expanding his mind, growing in understanding, learning from his environment, taking control of it and harnessing its resources to beneficial ends. But then came the seventh day, the day of rest, the day in which he was to put these other things aside in order to spend time sitting at the feet of his Maker. This is not to say that he would not have had fellowship with God on his work days, 'in the cool of the evening' perhaps (3:8), but on those days work was his principal and pleasurable activity. The seventh day, though, was to be the highlight of his week, the context in which all the rest of his activity had meaning and purpose, a day which he would spend in company with his God, his mind informed, his questions answered, growing in his knowledge of his Creator, and worshipping him. Thus both his work and his rest were to follow the pattern set by his Maker.

However, whatever one's views on this particular point, something needs to be said about rest in the form of refreshment after a week's labour. After all, the Fourth Commandment does mention the word 'labour' in work, which is the painful and irksome side of work which had not existed at creation. In Exodus 23:12 the observance of the Sabbath makes explicit mention of animals, servants and foreigners resting and being refreshed. The need is acknowledged. The Sabbath was intended as a relief from toil and labour. It therefore addressed the issue of the curse which God imposed upon creation following the fall of man into sin (Genesis 3:17-19). Though man must now labour in his work 'in the sweat of his brow' in a thorn-ridden world, God *still* appointed a day for his relief from this curse. There was still the gracious, compassionate provision made for him, though he had rebelled, to find rest. How was that rest to be found? By lying late in bed? By physical and mental inactivity? By sport? By entertainment? By self-indulgence? Of course not! Rather, by coming with a thankful heart to the God who had so lovingly made this provision, and finding refreshment in him. For these other things, however beneficial some of them may be in themselves, can never provide the refreshment that man most needs, and indeed often only substitute one form of oppression and weariness for another. Man needs rest: man needs God; and God has made provision for him in a way which surpasses all man's deserving.

One point more will be made on the subject of refreshment, for Exodus 31:17 says that God himself was refreshed in his rest on the seventh day after the work of the previous six (though it is not translated in this way in the NIV). Is this merely an anthropomorphism to help us mortals understand a use of the seventh day which actually has no corresponding reality in God who is Spirit? For God does not become weary (Isaiah 40:28) and so, we might conclude, does not need to be refreshed. Psalm 115:16 says that God has given the earth—the earth which he created—to the children of men. How then, at the end of creation, was God 'refreshed'?

The key to the meaning lies in his observation concerning all that he had made, that it was 'very good' (Genesis 1:31). He viewed his finished creation with delight and satisfaction, with the kind of refreshment which is associated with the pleasure of observing what has been done well and entering into the enjoyment of it. As the earth which he had made he had given to 'the children of men', whom he had also made, it follows that his enjoyment of his creation is bound up with his enjoyment of man, made in his own image, and made to have fellowship with him, as I said before. The refreshment God enjoyed at the completion of creation, and the refreshment he intends man to enjoy on the Sabbath, are therefore of the same kind. The essence of it is found in fellowship between God and man.

Our studies in the Old Testament in previous chapters have made the point about the universality of application of the Sabbath and there is no need to repeat the arguments here. That the Sabbath was made for man has been amply demonstrated. Were the rest of the Ten Commandments also made for man (for it is only the Sabbath which is under scrutiny here)? The answer must be in the affirmative. Paul in Romans writes of those who do not have the law, but they are still answerable to the law's requirements (Romans 2:12-16). Thus the law is universally applicable, and not limited to the Jews alone. Furthermore, Paul cites the law in other places showing its applicability to all men. One interesting example outside the Ten Commandments is that of not muzzling an ox while it is treading out the grain (1 Corinthians 9:9 and 1 Timothy 5:18, quoting Deuteronomy 25:4). In Ephesians 6:1-3, in enjoining obedience to parents upon children, he upholds the Fifth Commandment.

With the word 'Therefore' (Mark 2:28), Jesus draws a conclusion from his statement that 'The Sabbath was made for man, not man for the Sabbath.' This being the case, he asserts, it follows that he is also Lord of the Sabbath. Notice how he describes himself, as the Son of Man. As man, the Sabbath was made for his benefit as much as for any other man's; but as Lord of the Sabbath, he is saying that it is supremely his day.

Jesus, in the perfection of his sinless humanity, able to enjoy unbroken communion with his Father, declares that the Sabbath, far from having no relevance to him, or of his having no use for it, is in fact of special significance. He is its Lord. He is the ultimate reference point for our understanding of its meaning and place. Being Lord of the Sabbath did not mean, as some have supposed, that he could interpret it how he pleased or disregard it or redefine it if it suited him. 'I'm the boss here, I make the rules.' It was not like that, and that was not what he either said or meant. He had already demonstrated his lordship over creation and over Satan in his extensive ministry. He now says to the Pharisees that his lordship extends even to the Sabbath (which was their special sphere of interest!).

No command of God has ever been, or could ever be, replaced by anything which contradicted it. He does not command one thing one day, and another contradictory thing another day, as if he were indicating he had made a mistake which he is now rectifying. By asserting his lordship of the Sabbath, Jesus is not removing it, or replacing it, or modifying it, but upholding it. He always had been its Lord. Remember that on another occasion he said that not one jot or tittle would pass from the law until all was fulfilled, and warned about any who thought to do so (Matthew 5:17-20)! In the light of the strictures which follow it is almost ludicrous to imagine that Jesus was indicating that when the law had been fulfilled in his life then one might legitimately dispense with a jot or a tittle—or perhaps more! What he says ought to make us exceedingly cautious about suggesting that any aspect of the law no longer applies. For at that time Jesus said: 'Whoever therefore breaks one of the least of these commandments, and teaches men so, shall be called least in the kingdom of heaven; but whoever does and teaches them, he shall be called great in the kingdom of heaven. For I say to you, that unless your righteousness exceeds the righteousness of the scribes and Pharisees, you will by no means enter the kingdom of heaven.' There are people who seem to suggest that Jesus, being Lord of the Sabbath, had a right to reinterpret or redefine its use. In the light of what we have just read, that certainly is not the case!

Earlier in this chapter it was mentioned that some argue that Jesus reinterpreted the Sabbath law in much the same way as he reinterpreted the laws on adultery and murder in Matthew 5. This argument falls flat because Jesus did no such thing in connection with the laws on adultery and murder. He did not reinterpret them to give them a different meaning from what they had in the first place: he interpreted them in such a way as to draw out what they did mean from the beginning, applying them as they were intended to be applied. The only reinterpretation he was doing was that of the misinterpretation they had suffered at the hands of others!

Therefore when Jesus describes himself as being Lord of the Sabbath, he is certainly upholding the Sabbath principle, and he is also doing far more than that. Christians who seek to abrogate the Fourth Commandment from the statute book are seeking to remove something which has been made for them.

To those who argue that the Sabbath is a thing of the past, consider for a moment Jesus' own reasoning concerning his Father saying: 'I am the God of Abraham, the God of Isaac, and the God of Jacob' from which he concluded: 'He is not the God of the dead but of the living' (Matthew 22:32). Here he says: 'The Son of Man is also Lord of the Sabbath.' He is Lord of what abides, not of what is passing. He had just said, 'The Sabbath was made for man, not man for the Sabbath'. If it was made for him, predating Moses, then it is not superseded by the passing of the Mosaic covenant.

Whichever way we look at it, we always come round to the fact that the Sabbath principle is a continuing one. And because it is a continuing one, it is our responsibility correctly to interpret it. If we confess, 'Jesus is Lord', we are acknowledging his Lordship in every respect in which it is exercised, and if he says that he *is* Lord of the Sabbath, then it follows there *is* a Sabbath in which we are to recognize and honour his lordship.

A test case

We now come to the sequel to this confrontation with the Pharisees in the incident which took place in the synagogue, recorded in Matthew 12:9-14, Mark 3:1-6 and Luke 6:6-11. Luke informs us that this event took place on a different Sabbath from the previous incident (Luke 6:6), probably shortly afterwards. There 'happened' to be present a man with a withered hand. The scribes and Pharisees were so well aware of this (Luke 6:7) that one strongly suspects it to have been a 'set up job'. They were clearly more interested in what he would do about the man than they were in attending to his teaching, for they had planned their line of attack in advance. Indicating the man, they asked Jesus the question: 'Is it lawful to heal on the Sabbath?' (Matthew 12:10). But Jesus turned the tables upon the legalists in the question he returned to them: 'Is it lawful on the Sabbath to do good or to do evil, to save life or to kill?' (Mark 3:4).

This is strong stuff! Surely no one is talking about doing evil or destroying on the Sabbath? No? The Pharisees were doing evil by plotting to destroy Jesus (Matthew 12:14)—not on the Sabbath, of course! The way Jesus puts it highlights the issues involved. What was the preoccupation of the Pharisees? In doing good, in saving life? Not a bit of it. Their interest was in themselves, in lining their own nest; other people's problems were not their concern and they wouldn't lift a finger to help them (Matthew 23:4). Their self-interest clashed with God's interest, and, if our reading of the Gospels is correct, nowhere did it seem to come out more clearly and bitterly than on the Sabbath issue. Jesus is Lord of the Sabbath, but he was not their Lord. Consequently their view of the Sabbath was different from his, and when they saw his right use of the day they were filled with rage (Luke 6:11).

Mark remarks that Jesus looked round at them with anger, grieved by the hardness of their hearts (3:5). Basically, we are presented once again by need and the opportunity to meet it. By making a public example of the situation, Jesus further clarifies what the Sabbath is intended for, in so doing exposing the evil hearts of his opponents. They had interpreted the Sabbath purely in terms of what was *prohibited* by the law; Jesus is interpreting it in terms of what was *promoted* by the law. What matters is not what are you *not* going to do on the Sabbath, but what *are* you going to do?

Jesus' words about doing good or doing evil, about saving life or killing (Mark 3:4) are remarkably severe, presenting a stark contrast. He is not asking a question simply for his antagonists to answer. Not at all. His own response to the situation before him will be an answer to that very question. By doing the one thing he will not be doing the other, and he wants this to be understood by all. If he does not do good as far as the man in question is concerned, he is doing evil, for that which is good and which is within his power and opportunity to do for the man he would be withholding. To put it more starkly, he has a choice of saving a life or destroying a life—no middle way is permitted. These religious leaders were playing fast and loose with matters of life and death. They weren't concerned about the needs of men and women and meeting them, they had no compassion for this man with a withered hand (why do you think Luke draws attention to the fact that it was his *right* hand which was withered?). It did not enter their heads for a moment to give the man a helping hand (literally or metaphorically), only to use him to take the ground from beneath Jesus' feet. Yet again we are reminded that when it comes to law, if we don't understand the reason for which it is given we will abuse both its letter and its spirit.

'Is it lawful on the Sabbath to do good or to do evil, to save life or to kill?' You notice they could not or would not answer this question. 'Is it lawful to work on the Sabbath?' No, it is not. For the commandment says, 'In it you shall do no work.' But that is not the question Jesus asked. His question went behind the law to the principles upon which the law was established. It was an area in which they were not well versed! It has already been shown that in giving man the Sabbath, God had man's highest and ultimate good in view. The law is for man's good and intended to promote his welfare.

So it is lawful to do good on the Sabbath (did we doubt it?). Remember the context, though, which is that of promoting our relationship with our God through giving time and attention to his Word. It was of course lawful to do good on every day of the week (and it still is!). Take the modern example of a man who works as a garage mechanic all week but who has strong sabbatarian principles. A visiting family turn up at church one Sunday morning, and as they drive into the car park the bonnet of their car is suddenly enveloped in a spectacular cloud of steam. What is a talking point among the spectators is a cause of consternation and potentially great trouble to the visitors. What is the mechanic to do? 'I'll fix it tomorrow' is hardly an answer to encourage the family.

Surely the answer is obvious. 'Leave it to me. I know what the problem is and I can sort it out for you. You go in and enjoy the meeting.' Is this mechanic breaking his Sabbath principle? Is he who maintains the validity of the Fourth Commandment breaking it in order to meet the needs of this unfortunate family? Is this the famous 'exception which proves the rule'? Is it a case of: 'The commandment says this, but on this occasion I must do that'? It is nothing of the kind. The mechanic, though he may find himself doing the same *kind* of work on the Sabbath, is not doing his own work on the Sabbath. He has put aside his weekday work, as the commandment stipulates, in order to give himself to the things of

God, only as it happens he is called upon to use his skills in the cause of honouring the Lord on his day. The result is blessing to the family in that they can meet with God's people free from fretting concern and with thankfulness for his provision for their needs, and there is blessing to the man in question in the knowledge that the Lord has enabled him to be of service to others for Jesus' sake. This leads into the next point.

'Come back tomorrow'

Luke draws our attention to another Sabbath occasion (13:10-17) on which Jesus was teaching in a synagogue. While he was there, and perhaps while he was teaching, his eyes fell upon a woman who was bent double, quite unable to stand straight but compelled to look at the ground all her life. The narrative informs us that this condition was satanic in its origin, and that she had been like that for eighteen years. She was there, but we are not informed that she had come for the express purpose to be healed. Once again, it was Jesus who took the initiative, calling her to him. He had on a previous occasion in another place quoted Isaiah 61:1, declaring that this prophecy had been fulfilled in the people's hearing. For this woman on this occasion to be left in this condition would have been a rank contradiction of his mission. What difference, though, would a day make in eighteen years? The synagogue ruler may have thought he had a point when he said, 'There are six days on which men ought to work; therefore come and be healed on them, and not on the Sabbath day'! However, both his lack of respect for Jesus and his sidestepping the issue that Jesus was the one who had taken the initiative come over loud and clear. His comment should have been made to Jesus, but directing it instead toward the people to undermine Jesus' authority rather savours of cowardice as well as self-righteous indignation.

Now note very carefully how Jesus countered this argument. First of all he exposed the man's hypocrisy. By calling him a hypocrite (verse 15) he indicates that the man was 'acting a part'. This was a public confrontation which involved more than Jesus' own personal concern. Had the word been spoken against him personally, he might well have let it pass. But here was a man standing up and undermining something sacrosanct in the Sabbath principle. The ruler of the synagogue, indignant though he was (verse 14), was indignant from the wrong cause. Had he merely been troubled through having received wrong teaching himself, no doubt Jesus' answer to him would have been different. They had their hands on the law, but the law did not have its hands on them! Their heart was in the law, but the law was not in their hearts.

Jesus did not answer the man with invective. He rightly accused him, and he also gave such a simple explanation of what he had done that no one could have difficulty appreciating it. It is very similar to the explanation he gave on that other occasion when the man with the withered hand was healed (Matthew 12:11-12). Jesus said more than this, though. We should observe that the woman's first reaction was to glorify God (verse 13). We can imagine her stretching up with uplifted hands to God to honour him for his wonderful and undeserved kindness to her, in an attitude of which she had been utterly incapable for eighteen years. However, I was about to comment on what Jesus further said concerning her. For this woman, who was a 'daughter of Abraham' (verse 16), not only was an extra day of misery unnecessary, it was especially *appropriate* that she should be released from Satan's bondage on the Sabbath. Of all days, there was something especially fitting that the Sabbath should be the day on which a child of God should be brought back into fellowship with God. The objectors to the miracle would not have thought twice about leading their animals away to water them on the Sabbath, and here was the One providing living water on the Sabbath for a poor woman who had been suffering in a parched spiritual wilderness for years and years. Jesus was saying to the man, as well as to the congregation: 'This is what the Sabbath is all about.'

The principal use Jesus made of the Sabbath, certainly while he was in Galilee, was 'preaching the gospel of the kingdom' (Matthew 4:23) in the synagogues. His words at Mark 1:38-39 (and Luke 4:43-44) indicate not only that this happened, but that it was his mission and that his plan of campaign involved systematic coverage of the area (Mark 6:6b). Luke informs us (4:15-16) that, wherever he was on the Sabbath, it was his custom to go into the synagogue, read from the Scriptures, and preach to the people. Because of the restrictions imposed on travel in the land on the Sabbath, it may be that this was the day of the week when he was not besieged by huge crowds. Nevertheless, it is likely the synagogues would have been packed to capacity to hear him. His preaching was authoritative (Mark 1:22) and gracious (Luke 4:22). Its compelling nature—indeed, everything about it—caused astonishment among the people who had clearly never heard anything of the sort, and certainly not from the scribes (Mark 1:22). We are told that his teaching was such that he was 'glorified by all' (Luke 4:15). The substance of his teaching is captured in his quotation from Isaiah 61:1-2a when at Nazareth (Luke 4:18-19) because, as he said on that occasion, 'Today this Scripture is fulfilled in your hearing' (Luke 4:21). There is in these verses a strong hint at the year of jubilee which formed part of the law (Leviticus 25:8-17, especially verse 10) and yet which was seldom, if ever, observed.

However, the fulfilment of Isaiah's prophecy went far beyond even this, reaching deeper than simple outward restoration to freedom, addressing the issue of what is involved in the Lord's favour. The poor, the brokenhearted, the captives, the blind, the oppressed—what were these people doing in a nation who were called by God's name? The truth is that this had come about through the nation—meaning its people—being out of favour with their God. Jesus had come, he himself said, to proclaim and therefore to restore that favour. He had come to restore the broken relationship with God which was the root cause of these troubles and of every other irreversible tragic situation. He used the Sabbath day to bring people back into the enjoyment of what the Sabbath was intended to be: a time for communion with God, to learn of him, to rejoice in him, to glory in his grace with thanksgiving and praise. To be in his presence on the Sabbath was to be in the presence of God. Not all the people recognized this or made proper use of it, many having false expectations from him (for example the people of his home town of Nazareth—Luke 4:28), but those who witnessed his words and works 'rejoiced for all the glorious things that were done by him' (Luke 13:17).

Let us bear in mind that what Jesus was doing throughout was 'remembering the Sabbath day, to keep it holy' (Exodus 20:8). He who was 'born under the law' (Galatians 4:4) perfectly kept the law. So when he remembered the Sabbath day, he was doing so to perfection. We have seen that the opposition he frequently experienced on the Sabbath arose because he was keeping it as his Father intended, and as the law likewise indicated, he was doing so in an environment hostile to its purpose.

Jesus' use of the Sabbath was a practical demonstration of what it really meant to keep the Sabbath day holy. This is what his Father wanted, that with his divine heart of compassion he should bring the word concerning the kingdom of God to harassed and helpless people described as sheep without a shepherd (Matthew 9:35-36). We must conclude that this should be the primary object of preaching and a supremely appropriate use of the Sabbath honouring the Fourth Commandment. The exposition of God's Word by the power of the Holy Spirit is central to this because of the fact that his Word, whatever may be the content on any occasion, is always directed to the maintenance of a right relationship between Author and hearer. The Sabbath was rightly used in the proclamation and the hearing of the gospel and, naturally, in whatever was the appropriate response to the message, whether repentance and confession, or praise and thanksgiving, or prayer and intercession. All focused upon God meeting with his people in grace and his people fittingly responding.

In John 5:1-23 we read of the healing of the man who had an infirmity— presumably he was paralysed in some way—for 38 years, and who had been lying there at the Pool of Bethesda for quite some time. Because this healing took place on the Sabbath it provided a focus for controversy between Jesus and the Jewish leaders. Jesus had said to the man, 'Rise, take up your bed and walk' (verse 8). When confronted by the authorities who declared it was not lawful for him to do so, he quoted Jesus as having authorized it (verses 10-11). In response to the Jewish leaders' accusations that Jesus was doing work on the Sabbath, Jesus added fuel to their fire with what they took as a very provocative statement, but which actually is a very telling one: 'My Father has been working until now, and I have been working' (verse 17). It would seem that to their understanding, when Jesus spoke of his 'working until now' like his Father, he was including working on the Sabbath. They saw the day, they read the words of the law, they saw what they considered was his working on the Sabbath, and, *ergo*, he was breaking it!

So what did Jesus mean by his Father working 'until now' and likewise he himself working? This is the Lord of the Sabbath speaking. When did

God rest from his work? After the completion of the created order. But, Jesus maintains, God is working 'until now'. Why? Because (anticipating what will be said in a later chapter) man had yet to enter into the rest of fellowship with God intended by the rest of the seventh day. The work of creation is finished, yes, but the purpose for which it all exists has been marred by the sin of man and by the curse consequently imposed upon the entire created order. It is no mere chance that Jesus goes on to talk about the resurrection to eternal life and about judgement and condemnation (verses 19-30). It is all organically connected with the Sabbath. A great work is going on 'until this day', and it is the work of redemption, which must be completed in order to bring about the reconciliation of all things to himself (Colossians 1:20) and thereby introduce eternal life and the 'rest' promised to the people of God. When we have grasped this, we can see that Jesus legitimizes activity on the Sabbath which works to this grand end. It is, as the Puritans were later to call it, 'the market day of the soul'. What was Jesus doing on the Sabbath? He was very specifically preaching the gospel and particularly preparing people for a place in heaven and for full fellowship with his Father. This was what the Sabbath was all about, as we have observed in earlier chapters.

What was the Jews' interpretation of Jesus words in speaking of his working 'until now' (verses 17-18)? We read that the Jews sought to kill him, because he not only broke the Sabbath, but also said that God was his Father. So was he breaking the Sabbath, or was he not? What does the statement, 'he not only broke the Sabbath' convey to us? Naturally we have to take it along with the clause which accompanies it. There were two grounds upon which the Jews sought to kill him: firstly because he broke the Sabbath, secondly because he said that God was his Father. Both were considered grounds for the death penalty under Jewish law. If he was flagrantly a Sabbath breaker, their law said he must be executed (Exodus 31:14-15; 35:2); if he falsely claimed God to be his Father he was guilty of blasphemy and that also carried the death penalty (Leviticus 24:16). However, just as his claim upon God as being his Father was not blasphemous but perfectly true, so also his actions in respect of the Sabbath were absolutely and perfectly correct, and true to the requirement of the law. So the Jews were wrong on both counts.

Once again, what we see here is a conflict in interpretation. The interpretation of the Fourth Commandment by the Jewish leaders was defective and fault-finding because their hearts were defective and fault-finding! They saw a man carrying a 'burden'; they did not see a man relieved of an infinitely greater burden! What a delight to the man it must have been to be able to carry his bedding instead of being confined interminably to lie on it! Further, their jealousy and fear of Jesus shut out all possibility of his being who he said he was, even though the evidence was staring them in the face.

After the synagogue meeting in Capernaum when the demon-possessed man was restored on a Sabbath (Mark 1:21-28), Jesus and others went to the home of Simon and Andrew (verse 29). Simon's mother-in-law was laid up with a fever and of course they immediately told Jesus about her. We do not read of their requesting him to heal her. Maybe Simon simply explained that unfortunately his wife's mother would not be able to be with them because she was confined to bed with a fever. If so, Jesus could have left her, and probably the fever would have passed in time. But no, he took the initiative—and observe the gracious, sensitive and gentle way in which he did so, taking her by the hand and helping her up. Instantly she was completely well and strong again, and she doubtless rejoiced in being able to serve them instead of languishing uselessly on a bed of sickness. Jesus had made the Sabbath for her what it could not otherwise possibly have been, and as well as having the pleasure of serving him she would have had the opportunity to benefit from his instruction and example.

This, however, is not the end of the incident, for (verse 32) a great crowd gathered outside the door having brought the sick and demon-possessed to be healed. We note this took place after sunset, that is, when the Sabbath was over, for unlike our practice of the day being regarded as running from midnight to midnight, theirs ran from sundown to sundown. Thus this time-consuming ministry of healing took place after, not during, the Sabbath. Mark, by reference to the time, is careful to point this out. It was understood that Jesus kept the Sabbath, and this was in general respected by the people.

In fact there is no record of Jesus performing any extensive healing ministry on the Sabbath. Jesus, who had formerly engaged in the carpenter's trade, working six days and resting one as the law commanded, did not cease to follow the same pattern when he began his itinerant ministry. The work was different, but he still laboured in preaching and teaching, in healing the sick and casting out demons, in feeding great crowds and in stilling the storm, in nurturing his disciples, as he travelled from place to place. It is because Jesus kept the Sabbath that the Pharisees had so little material with which to accuse him of breaking it!

Three critical New Testament passages

In the New Testament there are three critical passages we must examine which may or may not touch upon the Sabbath: Romans 14:5, Galatians 4:10 and Colossians 2:16. It is especially important to understand these in context lest we put a construction on Paul's words which was never intended.

Whether the 'days' of Galatians 4:10 refers in any way to sabbaths is questionable. In writing of their 'observing' days and months and seasons and years, the word he uses indicates the giving of close attention to the details of these things, that is, concentrating on the minutiae. The way he puts it is entirely consistent with what he says throughout the letter, that their focus has shifted from reality to ritual, from a Person to a performance. The Old Testament ceremonial laws and national festivals to which he here refers in a general way had typological significance which found their terminal fulfilment in their existing form in the finished work of Christ (unlike the moral aspects of the law which, though fulfilled in a different sense in Christ or by Christ, continue to be valid in their existing form). Paul had in mind, firstly, the rules and regulations of Judaism in general which some of the Jews were trying to impose upon Gentiles; and, secondly, the legalistic manner of observing them, as if it was in the doing of these things that they would meet with God's approval. He stresses to the Gentiles of the Galatian churches that embracing Judaism is a step backwards and that dependence upon religious observances is a departure from Christ and a return to spiritual bondage (Galatians 4:9; 5:4).

Paul's concern is much the same in Colossians 2:16, only here he does include mention of the sabbath, or, to be more accurate, to 'sabbaths' in the plural. This is the only place in the whole of the New Testament from which anyone could even begin to attempt to make out a case for the cessation of the Sabbath. When the matter is examined in the light of the context, however, it is very difficult to support such an interpretation. For in this verse (and it is important that we should observe this) the apostle lumps together without discrimination food and drink, festivals, new moons and sabbaths. What is the common element which binds them all together? He explains in the next verse that they are a shadow of things to come, but that the substance, or the body, is Christ. They are not to worship the shadow, but the body! In this description he is therefore making it quite plain that he has the ritualistic aspects of the Old Testament law in view. It is this which is the common element. The Jews would have understood well enough from this, even by the very form of words he used, that the apostle was referring to the sacrifices and offerings which ordered and regulated the whole of their lives. The instructions of Numbers 28 and 29 are summarized in 2 Chronicles 2:4 by Solomon: 'I am building a temple for the name of the LORD my God, to dedicate it to him, to burn before him sweet incense, for the continual showbread, for the burnt offerings morning and evening, *on the Sabbaths, on the New Moons, and on the set feasts* of the LORD our God. This is an ordinance forever to Israel.' Nehemiah also employs the same formula of words when he refers to 'the regular burnt offering of the Sabbaths, the New Moons, and the set feasts' at a time when the nation drew up a covenant promising obedience to the LORD (Nehemiah 10:33).

Incidentally, it is worth noting that various Jewish commemorative events were regarded as 'sabbaths' or 'rests' even if they did not fall on the seventh day (see Leviticus 23).

The animal sacrifices which formed part of the Jews' way of life under the Old Testament dispensation no longer have any place now that Christ has come and fulfilled what they pointed forward to, even though the teaching about them is still instructive in a number of ways. The distinctive ceremonial practices in the form of animal sacrifices on the Jews' feast days and new moons and sabbaths had now passed into obsolescence, having served their purpose until the time when Christ came and offered himself once for all in dying upon the cross, and the Colossian church were not to allow Judaisers to intimidate them into taking up such obsolete practices.

Throughout this and the previous chapter the apostle is laying stress upon the pre-eminence of Christ (1:18; 2:9), the comprehensiveness of his accomplishments and the universality of his authority (1:16-20), and the fact that the believer is united with him (2:12), lives in him (2:6), is rooted in him and built up in him (2:7), and is complete in him (2:10). Paul cannot bear the thought that they might be cheated from the full enjoyment of all that this means. Indeed, there is not only the danger of ritual performances of a law which had been fulfilled in Christ, looking back at the law instead of from the law to Christ, but there is also the danger of being led astray in the opposite direction by practices based on supposed visions and other fanciful ideas (2:18). Law and—dare we say it—even visions also, may have their place, but it is when they are taken out of their proper place that they are misused and harm is done.

In short, in this section of his letter Paul has nothing to say about the Fourth Commandment, and his reference to sabbaths is simply a natural one on account of his argument concerning the rituals of the Old Testament law which took place on such days.

However, lest we become bogged down in technicalities, or, to change the metaphor, lest we miss the wood for the trees, remember that in these passages the thing which most concerns Paul is the danger of his readers subtly being enticed back into a legalistic way of life comprising 'do this' and 'don't do that', and into a formal religion which finds its security in the performance of ritual. Those who take a strong line on Sabbath observance today need this caution against the dangers of legalism, as do any who are fighting a cause, however just that cause may be. Law must always be viewed in the context of redemption. The law was given to a redeemed people (Exodus 20:2). The law points to Christ and leads to Christ (Galatians 3:24). The law is fulfilled in Christ in every sense of the word (Matthew 5:17). The righteous requirements of the law are fulfilled in us when we live in Christ and are led by the Spirit (Romans 8:4). Paul everywhere displays a high respect for the law and expects it to be honoured and rightly used, but the last thing he wants is for people to depend upon it, in either its moral or ceremonial aspects, as a means of salvation or even as a means of attaining a sense of personal satisfaction expressing itself in the thought: 'Haven't I done well!'

In the letter to the Romans Paul stresses that outward observance of the law, even the moral law which is still valid, is not the way of justification before God. He doesn't thereby invalidate the law, as he is at pains to point out. Coming finally to the passage in Romans 14:5, the apostle is dealing with problems thrown up by those who are weak in the faith. Whether he is indicating the Sabbath in this verse is open to question, though some seem to think he is. In this section there is a parallel case with those who will eat only vegetables. Such a one Paul describes as 'weak' in the faith (verses 1, 2). Only, in the case of the observance of the day, he does not indicate which of the two (if either) is the 'weaker' brother! He may even by this point have moved away from the idea of a weaker brother, though in view of what follows and the conclusion of 15:1 this is unlikely. Paul has already warned us in verse 1 to avoid disputing over disputable matters or, it may be, exercising judgements over matters of opinion. We have no right to force our opinions, however correct they may be, upon those who for the time being do not see things our way. How we like to have everything wrapped up, sealed into watertight compartments! We feel satisfied when we have got it all worked out, and upset when others will not toe the line! However, we have to face the fact that God has left some areas in which we are to reach our own conclusions based on the overall teaching of Scripture without his explicit legislation, and this often takes time as we progress toward maturity.

So here Paul presents us with two examples of matters in which there were differences of opinion within the church at Rome. He does not say either that the matters are unimportant in themselves or that it is unimportant what conclusions we reach about them; indeed he is careful to safeguard the order of the church either from the weak hijacking freedom of conduct within the church, or from the strong insensitively crushing the spirit of the conscience of the weak who have not yet come to a mature understanding of their freedom in Christ.

We might say that the actual cases cited by Paul are poles apart, and in a sense they are. On the whole, what people will and will not eat on principle may seem to us to be of relatively little importance, though if we compare this passage with 1 Corinthians 8:13 and 1 Corinthians 10:25 (both taken in context) it is likely that the scruples of those who would not eat meat lay in the fact that most meat bought in the market had previously been offered up to Roman idols. For them it was a live issue. Their argument went that by eating they would be either participating in idol worship or condoning or supporting or encouraging it. Though that was not actually the case, said Paul, they nevertheless had to be sensitive to the consciences of those who thought it to be so. It takes only a moment's thought to see how this kind of problem manifests itself in all sorts of guises in society—for example, should Christians abstain from any form of alcoholic beverage on the ground that their drinking might be wrongly construed by people who have a very different attitude toward alcohol; or is it giving support to what some see as a largely corrupt drinks industry?

The case of the one observing the day and the one not doing so is undoubtedly more difficult. However, both are covered by two caveats: firstly that neither is to judge the other, and secondly the proviso being understood that both are seeking to honour the Lord. On this occasion Paul is not addressing people who are out to serve their own interests but those who are serious in their determination to please the Lord. This is good, but what often arises from the earnestness of such people is, firstly, concern about the potential moral implications of things they do or do not do, and, secondly, concern about how others respond to the same things. Thus the eating of meat is not the problem, for that is quite legitimate and is not a moral issue; but, because the meat had probably first been offered to an idol before being sold in the market, there might be moral implications in eating it. And so, secondly, there is the potential for those who have reached certain conclusions about these things to look askance at others who take a different line.

When we appreciate that Paul is discussing the 'moral implications' issue in this chapter we see that the matter of observing or not observing the day falls into the same category. 'Should I do this, or shouldn't I? If I do, am I doing wrong because of X, and if I don't, am I at fault because of Y?'

For this reason it is very hard, if not impossible, to conceive that the apostle was thinking of the weekly Sabbath at all. Sabbath observance was so deeply embedded in the minds of Jews, whether Christians or not, that had there been any question about it Paul would have written in unmistakable terms. That was not a 'moral implications' issue. Much more likely is that, because he was writing to a church comprised largely of Gentiles, he had in mind the Jews among them who felt they should be still observing the special feast days specified in their law. After all, they were still Jews, and so what right had they to discard these requirements, even though they were now Christians, and even though the majority in the church were unaffected by these things? On the other hand, some among them might happily have dispensed with these feast days without any qualms, arguing that they were free to do so without risk to their Jewishness or compromise to their obedience to the Lord.

In a nutshell, the matter of eating meat was one which probably affected principally the Gentile believers on account of the background out of which they had been converted, while the matter of observing days was one which concerned the Jewish Christians because of their national heritage as God's covenant people and the whole of the law which went with it. For the Gentiles, some felt free to eat meat without questioning its source; others could not in good conscience do so. For the Jews, some drew the line and left the traditions behind; others believed they should maintain them.

Paul handles both cases as one, recognizing that there are matters on which believers may come to different conclusions and that the response on each side toward the other should be that of gracious acceptance and respect, while the focus of all should be on 'righteousness and peace and joy in the Holy Spirit. For he who serves Christ in these things is acceptable to God and approved by men' (verse 18).

The apostle's treatment of the matter is clearly very different from how he wrote to the Galatian and Colossian churches. The churches of Galatia were turning back to reliance upon ritual, and the church at Colosse was being troubled by those who sought to turn them in the same direction. Paul was incisive in his condemnation of such practices. Here in Romans, though, the situation is quite different because, whether weak or strong, the believers were seeking to honour God in what they did or did not do, and their reliance was entirely on Christ. It was not a matter of right or wrong, calling for rebuke and correction.

In summary, none of these passages really has anything definitive to say about the Fourth Commandment. Our understanding must therefore continue to rest upon what we have learned so far from elsewhere in God's Word where the teaching is clear and unmistakable.

The Sabbath rest of Hebrews 4

One passage remains to be considered from the New Testament which turns out to be considerably more important than might at first sight be supposed. However, there appears to be widespread confusion about the meaning of Hebrews 4.[6] For this reason we must spend some time in its exegesis. We need carefully to prepare the way toward a correct understanding of this passage. Because of the existence of a variety of interpretations it will be necessary to point out what the passage is not saying as well as what it is. As with any other portion of God's Word it is not what we think which matters, but what God has said. We need to understand him, and when we come to passages which we find difficult, we need always to remember that the problem lies with the reader, not with the Author! The deficiency is not in the way God has communicated what he wants to say, but ours in failing to hear him as we ought! Experience teaches us that there can be a host of reasons for this—inadequate knowledge, spiritual immaturity, imperfect theology, wishful thinking, lack of serious devotion and submission to him, to name but a few. Treat this as a test passage, if you like, and remember—to reiterate what has just been said—what matters is not what I might be setting forth, but what God's Word actually says.

Let us examine this section first of all in the context of the overall purpose of the letter as a whole, and then in the context of the argument which more immediately surrounds it.

It does not take long for a student of the letter to the Hebrews to discover the complexity and intricacy of the arguments which are interwoven as the writer develops his subject, which is an expansion of his introductory statement in the first three verses of the opening chapter: 'God, who at various times and in various ways spoke in time past to the fathers by the prophets, has in these last days spoken to us by his Son, whom he has appointed heir of all things, through whom also he made the worlds; who being the brightness of his glory and the express image of his person, and upholding all things by the word of his power, when he had by himself purged our sins, sat down at the right hand of the Majesty on high.'

What an amazing introduction! How packed it is with statements inviting explanation! And that is exactly what the writer does as he proceeds. If we would understand the book we must look at every aspect of it from this reference point and never lose sight of it. He demonstrates the surpassing excellence of God's Son, whom he sent into the world, by means of a number of comparisons, the first being made with the angels. He shows from Scripture just how much the glory of the Son surpasses that of the angels. They, he says, for all their glory, are merely servants to those who will inherit salvation, but Jesus is the one who provides that salvation. They are created beings, he is the eternal Son.

Our purpose, however, is only to point out this feature, not to enlarge on it. As the letter unfolds, further comparisons are made. Perhaps even the word 'comparisons' gives the wrong impression, because the writer is intending not so much to compare Jesus with the angels, or with Moses, or with Aaron, as to introduce these people and the nature of their service to God as a witness to the fact that the *effectual* work was actually performed by the Son. So, for example, Moses served faithfully, but what he introduced under God, great though that was, was not an end in itself but a testimony to what was to follow (3:5), namely to the work that Jesus would accomplish.

However, some comparisons are immediate and direct, such as these:

'Of the angels he says…' (1:7)	'But to the Son he says…' (1:8)
'They will perish, …	but you remain' (1:11)
'They will be changed…	But you are the same' (1:12)
'…We do not yet see all things put under him [man]' (2:8)	'But we see Jesus … crowned…' (2:9)
'Moses was faithful in all his [God's] house' (3:5)	'But Christ as a Son over his own house' (3:6)

'There were many priests, because they were prevented by death from continuing' (7:23)	'But he, because he continues forever, has an unchangeable priesthood' (7:24)
'The law appoints …	but the word of the oath … appoints' (7:28)
'The priests … serve the copy and shadow' (8:4-5)	'But now he has obtained a more excellent ministry' (8:6)
'And every priest stands ministering daily and offering repeatedly the same sacrifices, which can never take away sins' (10:11)	'But this Man, after he had offered one sacrifice for sins forever, sat down at the right hand of God' (10:12—recalling 1:3)

This last one presents a more extended comparison and contrast, but in other cases the comparisons are even more detailed and complex, such as (to take just one example) that in chapter 9 between the earthly sanctuary and its service with all its limitations administered by the Aaronic priesthood, and the heavenly one presided over and administered by Christ.

Throughout the letter the writer is in effect saying to his readers: 'Look at this…' in relation to limitations or deficiencies, whether in the angels, or in man, or in the law, or in the sanctuary worship …. And then, while they are considering these things he adds: 'Now look at Jesus' in respect to the completeness, the comprehensiveness, the total effectiveness of all that he has accomplished in living, dying, rising again and ascending to his Father's right hand. If we fail to see Jesus at every turn in his argument we are missing the point of what he is telling us.

Another thing the writer does as the letter unfolds is to introduce a subject and then apparently to digress before taking it up again. For example, he introduces the high priestly ministry of the Lord Jesus Christ at the end of chapter 2 and the beginning of chapter 3, and then seems to break off until 4:14. He does the same with Melchisedek whom he mentions almost in passing (as we suppose) in 5:6, and we do not realize until the end of chapter 6 that he actually has a great deal more to say about him. In each case the 'digression' is there to prepare the way for what he intends to say more fully afterwards. In the latter case, speaking of the nature of the priesthood of Jesus, he develops a profound argument centred upon the words of Psalm 110:4.

Throughout these chapters, from 2:10 to 10:25 the writer is concerned principally with the many aspects of the high priesthood of Jesus; but he never allows the reader to stray into the realms of mere theology, for he confronts him at every turn with the need of application to his own situation. So in chapter 3, after telling his readers to consider the Apostle and High Priest of our confession (3:1) who is 'bringing many sons to glory' (2:10), before developing his teaching about the high priesthood of Jesus he spells out some home truths about the need to be 'brought to glory' and what it means, alluding to the wilderness travels and drawing a parallel with the Christian's present condition in the world.

For this purpose Psalm 95:7-11 forms the basis of a very interesting argument whereby the writer proves that the 'rest' promised to the people of God has yet to be realized. This is what we are now going to study, and it must begin with a careful reading of Hebrews 3:7 to 4:10.

Deuteronomy 1:34-35 refers to the 'oath' God took which deprived the people from entry into the 'good land', whereas Psalm 95:11 quotes this as depriving the people of the promised 'rest'. It is not a misquotation but an accurate expansion of the meaning. The Lord had promised 'rest' to Moses (Exodus 33:14), while Deuteronomy 12:9-10 speaks of 'rest' in the land of inheritance for the Israelite nation. This 'rest', however, was never intended to be anything other than the kind of rest which is obtainable only in the presence of the Lord. The rest was not in the land. It was to be a good land only so long as the blessing of God rested upon it. Without his blessing, it became a barren land. No, the rest was not in the land itself, but it was intended to be in the LORD, in the land. What made the place a place of rest was the presence of God, and nothing else. Moses saw this when he replied to the Lord: 'If your presence does not go with us, do not bring us up from here' (Exodus 33:15). The presence of God meant everything, and for Moses the lack of his presence was too terrible to contemplate. The blessings of God, whatever they may be, cannot be had or enjoyed without the presence of God.

This was the problem with the Israelites in the desert: they had an evil heart of unbelief which *departed from* the living God (Hebrews 3:12). The ultimate blessing promised them had been to enter his rest, but they could not do so without his presence, as they proved to their cost. We cannot have the gifts without the Giver. We cannot have this rest without the One in whom alone it is to be found.

In the passage under consideration, the writer of the letter to the Hebrews has been majoring on those who were not able to enter God's rest 3:11,18; 4:3,5,8). When he mentions this 'rest' for about the fourth time in 4:3, he suddenly refers back to creation as he adds: 'although the works were finished from the foundation of the world'. Here John Owen, in his great treatise on the Epistle to the Hebrews, observes: 'I do acknowledge that these words, as they relate to the preceding and ensuing discourses of the apostle, are attended with great difficulties; for the manner of the ratiocination [that is, the logical and methodical reasoning] or arguing here used seems to be exceedingly perplexed.'[7] The questions to be considered, then, are, firstly, why is there this sudden reference back to creation; and, secondly, what has it to do with the overall argument?

Firstly, then, what has the rest promised to the Israelites who were delivered from Egypt got to do with creation? This allusion to the seventh day of creation takes us right back to what the 'rest' is all about. Here we have just been considering the Israelites in the desert, depriving themselves, through rebellious unbelief, certainly of entry into the promised land, and, by implication, of entry into the promised rest. But when was that rest first made available? When was it first made possible to enter into it? God's rest, the writer reminds us, predates the wilderness wanderings, for it dates right back to the seventh day of creation, and it was a rest into which man was invited, to be entered into and enjoyed by him in his Maker's presence. Adam and Eve rejected God's word to them in favour of Satan's, shrank from their Maker in fear, and bore the penalty of their disobedience by being driven from the presence of God in the Garden of Eden. Insofar as they disobeyed their Maker and were ejected from the garden, they did not enter his rest. The 'rest' was there to be entered, but man through unbelief and disobedience did not enter it. The same was true for the Israelites in the desert under Moses. They were supposed to go into the land of promise *with God*. But they departed from the living God (3:10b,12) and so could not enter his rest (3:11). The writer is telling us that it is exactly the same 'rest' as was originally spoken of. It had a physical aspect insofar as it related to the land of Canaan, but its principal aspect was to have been the presence of God among them.

To say that the Sabbath of rest was clearly undermined is grossly to understate the case—it was *devastated* by the entry of sin into the world. In the garden Adam and Eve hid from God—fellowship had been broken. Restoration of this relationship has been in view in God's redemptive purposes ever since, and Hebrews 4 is addressing this very point.

Although God had completed his work of creation ('the works', verse 3) in six days and designated the seventh for man's immeasurable blessing in his transcendently blissful holy presence, the record stands that generation after generation since then people failed to enter his rest, the reason being their unbelief.

But, someone says, after the wilderness wanderings the next generation of Israelites did enter, under Joshua, did they not? So does that not wrap up the whole thing and close the chapter? No, says the writer. If you think Joshua had given the people rest (4:8), think again. For had that been the case the inspired writer of Psalm 95 would not have needed to put out a call to his own people 'Today' in connection with entry into God's rest. This rest, he says, is still here to be entered into *today*: don't be like that unbelieving generation who forfeited it. The psalm, which is evidently all about entering God's rest, is equally all about entering his *presence* (verses 2, 6). The two, as was asserted before, are inseparable. So the promised rest not only predates the deliverance from Egypt under Moses, it also postdates the entry into the land of promise under Joshua. The rest remains (verse 9) and the promise of entering it remains, too (verse 1).

The key to unlocking this passage is in recognizing that the writer is not talking about different 'rests' at different points in history, but has in mind essentially the same 'rest' throughout. The settings were different, whether at creation, or in the wilderness wanderings, or at the time and place of the psalm being written, or where and when the writer, whoever he was, penned his letter. It is all about something which is accessible by faith but forfeited by unbelief. That applied to Adam and Eve, to the Israelites in the desert, to those the psalm addressed, to the first readers of the letter to the Hebrews—and it applies equally to its more recent readers!

When Israel went into the land of promise under Joshua they had first of all to conquer it. The conquest involved not only annihilating all God's enemies in the land but also removing every last vestige of the corrupting influences of idolatry that were to be found there (see Deuteronomy 7:1-6). As we know, this did not happen, the book of Judges revealing only too clearly that the conquest was but partial in both respects. So there can be no doubt that Joshua did not give them rest. Though there is mention of 'rest' in Joshua 21:44 and 22:4, in the light of the context and also Joshua 11:23, it refers to rest from war—and Joshua is careful to acknowledge that it was not he who had given it, but the LORD. The same applies in Deuteronomy 12:9-10.

Anticipating what is going to be demonstrated later, observe that what Joshua, and the people with him, failed to achieve in a limited sense for their generation and succeeding ones, Jesus has accomplished completely for all his people for all time, conquering every enemy to present a perfect and prepared people into a perfect and prepared world.

Had Adam and Eve heeded God's word to them instead of entertaining Satan's deceitful ploy they would certainly have entered God's rest. Had the Israelites taken God at his word (and in view of all the miracles in Egypt they had every encouragement to do so) and therefore believed that he could and would bring them into the land of promise, all would have been well. But they hardened their hearts and so did not themselves enter the land God had conditionally promised them; only their children did.

Psalm 95 addresses the Israelites generations later, warning them to listen to and heed the voice of God. They, the psalmist says referring back, did not enter God's rest, and the same will apply to you, he adds, if you act in the same way that they did. But where were the Israelites when the psalm was written? Were they not in the promised land? Indeed they were. So how could the same possibly apply to them if the reference had been only to the land itself? Of course, it had not been to this. The issue had never been simply about living in the land, but about hearing and heeding the voice of God. That is why for the psalmist it was not a dead issue concerning generations back, but a live one concerning 'Today'.

The psalm, though it comprises two extraordinarily contrasting parts, is nevertheless a unit. As the writer calls others to come into the presence of God and joyfully to worship him, and as he thinks of abiding in his presence, indeed *resting* in his presence, under his protective care (verse 7), it is almost as if suddenly his heart is in his mouth with shock as the thought comes to him of the sheer awfulness of it being otherwise, as it had been with the Israelites in the wilderness; and then God speaks through him to warn the present hearers of the enormity of what they would be forfeiting if they turned away from him in their hearts. Surely any child of God who has spent time in the Father's presence must have some sense of horror that anyone should fly in the face of all the evidence and spurn such love?

The writer to the Hebrews says that the issue is still a live one for his own readers, centring upon their response to the gospel (4:2). Indeed, it is vitally connected with the rest of the seventh day of creation (4:4,5), identified in the time of Moses with the Sabbath of the Fourth Commandment. The writer of Hebrews makes this abundantly clear when he comes to 4:9, although this is lost in some of the English translations. The interesting and significant thing throughout this passage in Hebrews is that the Greek word for 'rest' in chapters 3 and 4 is always the ordinary one (*katapausis*, which means a place of resting down, of cessation). Yet as he concludes this part of his argument he uses—indeed it might be said he coins—another word, *sabbatismos*. Why, having used the other word consistently throughout the argument, does he now introduce a new one? I suggest there is only one reason, which is that he wishes very specifically to draw attention to the Sabbath, because it is the *sabbath* rest which is both the climax and the focal point of his argument. It is a *Sabbath* rest which remains for the people of God, as the NIV accurately describes it. There is something about the Sabbath, he says, of enduring significance and importance from the creation of the world right through to the time when Christ will come again. This 'sabbath-rest' remains, for God's people, and if it remains and is thus described in terms of the Sabbath, that word being emphasised, then it is vital that God's people should have a good understanding of what it means. So important is this to our whole destiny that we lose the concept of the Sabbath at our own peril.

A problem of translation and interpretation

In order to do justice to this passage from the letter it must be expounded yet a little more fully. Regrettably there have been various and differing interpretations of this section which only serve to show that some must have misunderstood it. I submit that a correct interpretation must be fully in accord with the rest of Scripture as well as making good sense in its own context. We have already observed that the writer of Hebrews sets out to prove that Christ is the one to whom we must look, for it is he alone who has accomplished redemption, having 'by himself purged our sins' (1:3), and who now sits enthroned at the right hand of his Father as our great High Priest. Where, though, does he feature in this present passage, from 3:7 to 4:13? What has all this to do with what Jesus has accomplished? What relevance has this passage to the overall argument? If we cannot see Jesus here, either we have somehow lost our way or the writer has lost the thread of his discourse.

Back in 2:5-9 the writer, quoting from another psalm, shows that whereas at creation all things were put in subjection under man (Psalm 8:6; Genesis 1:26-28), at present there is very clearly a serious shortfall in his dominion. In other words, somewhere along the line man has failed. This is just another manifestation of how far short man has fallen of all that God intended for him. This is what we see, or rather, do not see (2:8). But, by contrast, what we *do* see is that Jesus has not failed: far from it, he is crowned now with glory and honour, and there is no shortfall in his dominion. Not only so, but by his suffering of death he has accomplished this for his people (he being the captain of their salvation, 2:10), so that what he has already achieved his people will enter into through him. There is a 'not yet' as far as his people are concerned, but a 'now' as far as he is concerned.

The same applies in chapter 4, concerning the 'rest'. If we look at verse 1, we see the promise remains of entering his rest, and see that at verse 11 we are urged to make every effort to enter it. The implication therefore is that we have not yet entered it. Verses 6 and 9 indicate that it is there to be entered, and that some will enter it. But who, and how?

As to the 'who', verse 9 supplies the answer: the people of God. As to the 'how', verse 3 informs us that it is by faith, that is, by believing the gospel (verse 2). The writer declares, including himself among those who have believed: 'We enter that rest' (verse 3). He does not say, 'We have entered', but 'We enter…', or, 'We do enter…,' using language appropriate to the case. It is something which has not yet happened, but which is certain to happen on account of the promise of God coupled with faith in that promise (verse 2). This is not to deny that the people of God have a foretaste of it. The foretaste, though, only increases longing in anticipation of fulfilment.

This brings us to verse 10, which unfortunately has been incorrectly translated in the New International Version (presumably on the basis of aiming for consistency with what has gone before while under a misapprehension of the writer's argument). After the admirably clear and bold translation of verse 9, 'There remains a Sabbath-rest for the people of God', the NIV continues: 'for anyone who enters God's rest also rests from his own work, just as God did from his.' However, the tense in the original is different, because it refers to one *having entered*, and *rested*. Furthermore, it does not refer to 'anyone' but to 'the one', and does not specifically mention 'God's' rest, but 'his' rest. So more accurately it should be rendered: 'For the one having entered into his rest also himself rested from his works [that is, his own works], as God did from his.'

Using the NIV translation of verse 10, and bearing in mind that the writer has just mentioned the Sabbath-rest, the statement appears clear enough. God rested after his work of creation was finished and blessed the Sabbath day to man, and when man comes to the Sabbath he rests from *his* work, in much the same way as God did from his. The problem, though, is that while this statement might be true and indeed obvious, it does not fit in any way into the writer's argument.

However, the NIV translation, while it might be described as a legitimate attempt at continuity, is not actually what the Greek says. Much translation is heavily dependent upon context, and it would seem the NIV translators have relied upon a particular interpretation of the context to lead them to the statement: 'For *anyone* who enters *God's* rest also rests from his own work, just as God did from his.' The Greek, though, simply says, 'For *he* having entered *his* rest has himself also ceased from his works as God did from his'.

For the sake of clarity, here are the two translations of verse 10 side by side and phrase by phrase to highlight the differences, the NIV on the left:

For anyone	For he
who enters	having entered
God's rest	his rest
also rests	has himself also ceased
from his own work,	from his works
just as God did from his.	as God did from his.

Written like this, it becomes obvious that there are significant differences in virtually every line. But what do they really amount to? The NIV, by saying 'anyone' is indicating just *anyone*! And the rest indicated is *God's* rest. However, the original, which says '*He* having entered *his* rest', is indicating a person in the singular. Furthermore, it is not necessarily *God's* rest that he is said to have entered, for it could be his *own* rest.

All the way through the letter the writer consistently refers to his readers in the plural. Why therefore use the singular here if he is still referring to them? There is no real warrant for it. No, he really is referring to a singular person, that is, to one person in particular, which is Christ, even though at first sight it seems he is not actually mentioned by name.

Written the way the NIV puts it, the verse makes no sense, because it does not fit the writer's argument. We know that all the way through the letter the writer is demonstrating the superiority of the accomplishments of Christ over and above all his forerunners. Christ is greater than the angels, Christ is superior to Moses, Christ excels the high priests, he is greater than Abraham, and so on. Well, here we have just been reading about Joshua (4:8) not giving the people rest. Who then, we ask, *has* given them rest? The question is *not* left unanswered, it is not left mysteriously hanging in the air, as it would be if we followed the NIV translation. Not at all: there remains a rest for the people of God, a *sabbatismos*, the *true* rest as enshrined in the Sabbath, and the one who has given it is he who has entered into his rest, namely Jesus.

Then there is another difference, which lies in the problem of tense. The NIV says, 'For anyone who *enters* God's rest also *rests* from his own work', whereas the original says, 'For the one *having entered* into his rest also himself *rested* from his works', indicating something which *has* taken place, in contrast with, and in the context of, what has *not* yet taken place. So the writer, having said in verse 9 that the Sabbath-rest still remains for God's people, yet to be entered into, says in verse 10 that one *has* entered into it, on the basis of which, in verse 11, he exhorts *us* to make every effort ourselves to enter into it.

Note too the *comparison* which is made in verse 10, expressed in the words: 'as God did from his'. In *just the same way* as God has ceased from his works—namely the works of creation—someone has also ceased from *his* works. Those who say the reference is to people ceasing from striving by their own works to obtain salvation have no foundation whatsoever for their argument, because the passage nowhere refers to anyone striving by their works to obtain salvation—that is simply not the matter under consideration. The argument is about obedience and disobedience, between belief and unbelief. Then again, to compare a sinner ceasing from trusting in his own works for salvation with God ceasing from his works of creating the world is actually rather ludicrous. What we have in this verse is what we might call a *worthy* or *just* or *appropriate* comparison, firstly in respect of the *persons* being compared, and secondly in respect of the *works* being compared. The only just comparisons are between the Son and the Father, and between redemption and creation. Christ is seated at his Father's right hand, having completed *redemption's work*, and therefore having ceased from his works, having 'by himself purged our sins' (1:3). The writer is, here as everywhere else in his letter, working out his grand theme on the glories of the risen and ascended Christ.

If the believer had already entered this rest there would be no need for the following exhortation to do so. The writer does not say in verse 11, 'Make sure that you really have entered that rest', but, in effect, 'Make sure that you really are going to be there' (compare Paul's similarly implied exhortation in Colossians 1:23). The Israelites who left Egypt looked as if they were going into the promised land, but they didn't get there, and they didn't get there because they didn't believe and act upon the promise God gave them.

In view of the whole purpose of this letter, verse 10 is capable of only one meaning. One *has* entered that rest, and that one is Jesus. He came to do the work his Father gave him (John 4:34), and this work he accomplished (Hebrews 1:3). As surely as his Father finished his work of creation and rested on the seventh day, so Jesus finished his work of redemption and has entered his rest. Again, where man in general has failed, Jesus has succeeded. And he has succeeded in order to take his people in (2:10).

We see therefore that this rest has nothing whatever to do with man's works, or his striving after salvation (for the context has nothing whatever to do with such a concept), but has everything to do with Jesus' work, *finished*, thereupon entering into his rest. We are not considering just 'anyone', but Jesus! And we are required to believe and act upon the promises of God, 'For all the promises of God in Him are Yes, and in Him Amen' (2 Corinthians 1:20).

There would be no need for the writer to exhort his readers to 'make every effort' to enter God's rest (4:11) if they were already believers and had already entered it having ceased from their own efforts to get there. It simply wouldn't make sense. The *effort* required is the striving of faith, in contrast to the example of the disobedience of unbelief. Hebrews 4:3 says that by faith 'we enter' into rest. It doesn't say we 'have entered' into it, because it does not denote a completed action. Neither does it say we 'will enter' into it as if it is something entirely future. The wording is exactly appropriate to our present condition as believers living by faith in Christ, and it is somewhat akin to our salvation: we have been saved, we are being saved, we will be saved. Our salvation is nearer now than when we first believed (Romans 13:11). There are past, present and future aspects to it. But whereas verse 3 says that we who believe *do* enter his rest, verse 10 speaks of one who *has* entered his rest. We *do*, because he *has*. He has secured for us by his obedience, even to the death of the cross, what we forfeited by our disobedience. It is just the same kind of argument as in 2:8-9 where, concerning man, 'we do not yet see all things put under him', whereas concerning Christ, 'but we see Jesus ... crowned with glory and honour'.

But, someone objects, why does the writer not name Jesus at this point? The answer is quite simply that there is no need to! When we grasp what he is communicating throughout this letter it should be self-evident here that the 'he' of verse 10 can refer to no one else. Later, in 10:5, the writer again (in the original!) says 'He', without naming Jesus: 'When *he* came into the world…'. But we don't stop to ask who the 'he' is, even though the quotation is from a psalm of David (Psalm 40:6). We understand from the context that the 'he' refers not to David but to Jesus. So, returning to 4:10, the same is true here.

Let us pick up the argument once more. We know the people under Moses did not enter God's rest foreshadowed in the promised land, and we know the reasons for this. We know, on account of the inspired psalmist's words (Psalm 95:7-11 quoted here) that Joshua had not really given the people rest, though he had successfully brought them into Canaan (verse 8). We know that the rest still remained to be entered (verse 9), and we are now enlightened as to its true nature in the 'sabbatismos'.

Now suppose the text went straight on to verse 11 from verses 8 and 9 (omitting verse 10), saying:

> 'For if Joshua had given them rest, then he would not afterward have spoken of another day. There remains therefore a rest for the people of God … Let us therefore be diligent to enter that rest….'

The writer has just been presenting us with an extensive catalogue of failure. How then can we be sure that we 'do' enter, or 'shall' enter, and that we will not simply follow in the tradition of failure (for even Joshua had not given them rest)? You see, do you not, how important verse 10 is to the argument? We can be sure only because *he has* entered. Where man failed, he has succeeded. But, as is affirmed throughout this letter, not only has he succeeded, he has succeeded *for us*. Our Great High Priest is actually still under view even though the writer appears for a moment to have digressed from this subject. We are to be diligent, or to strive, or to make every effort, to enter this rest. That is true, but it is not on the basis of the inadequacy of our own works. Not at all. It is solely on the basis of Christ's finished work!

To this there is to be added one final exegetical argument. All the way through the letter the writer interjects applicatory exhortations of various kinds to his readers. He wants them to keep their feet on the ground but also to keep them on their toes! And so he warns them, cautions them, urges them, encourages them, with whatever is appropriate as he develops his grand theme. Here in chapter 4, verses 11-13 are just one such exhortation, rather like a parenthesis, so that verse 14 in fact carries on logically from verse 10. If we so read it, recognizing its continuity, it should be even more clear that verse 10 is speaking of Jesus, and that he is indeed named after all, contrary to what might have been supposed earlier:

> 'There remains therefore a Sabbath-rest for the people of God. For he who has entered his rest has himself also ceased from his works as God did from his. … Seeing then that we have a great High Priest who has passed through the heavens, Jesus the Son of God, let us hold fast our confession.'

Having introduced Christ Jesus as 'the Apostle and High Priest of our confession' (3:1) he is now in a position to say this further of him, that he has 'passed through the heavens', a statement which hinges upon his having entered his rest and could not be made here without it.

So, from 3:7 and on into chapter 4 we are holding our breath with the question, 'Where does Jesus come into all this?' We know the passage must have him in mind all along, and we are waiting for his appearing again, the more so as the failure of so many to enter God's rest and the fact that Joshua didn't provide it leaves us with a sense of unease! If we appreciate the argument in context there can be no mistaking Jesus, who has entered his rest, having completed his works—his work of redemption in its every aspect, just as God his Father rested upon completion of creation's work.

When Moses sent out the spies into Canaan, they *went through the land* before bringing back their report with a view to taking possession (or so it should have been, Numbers 13:21). Later, the men Joshua sent out similarly *went through the land* to survey it prior to its division for inheritance purposes (Joshua 18:4). So Jesus has 'passed through the heavens', indicating his entering and as it were taking possession. This is no toe-hold hopefully to be extended, but complete possession! Jesus has not *begun* his rest, he has *entered* it! In him, we also enter, fully and completely, into the rest which God has prepared for those who love him.

Heaven and rest

This leads into one final area of potential confusion which needs clarification, because it seems to me that the 'rest' of Hebrews 4 is often identified with heaven, and that verse 9 is referring to heaven, the 'rest' being an eternal rest. This is not really so. It would be more accurate to regard it as a matter of association rather than identification. For though it is true that we will not fully enter our rest until we are in heaven, so that the two cannot be separated, they are nevertheless not one and the same. I commented earlier in this chapter that the rest was not in the land itself, but was intended to be in the LORD, in the land. What made the place a place of rest was the presence of God, and nothing else. 'Rest' and 'inheritance' are therefore, as their names suggest, different things and should not be confused. The Israelites were brought into the land of their inheritance given by God, yet often they had little rest in it. Why so? It is because their relationship with God was lacking. They could enjoy their inheritance only as long as they took delight in the One who had provided it for them.

By the grace and mercy of God, we who believe have been born again into a living relationship with him through Jesus Christ, and as a consequence have an inheritance reserved and waiting for us (1 Peter 1:4), an inheritance the writer of Hebrews refers to in Hebrews 9:15. When he says at 4:11 that we should 'be diligent to enter that rest' his primary concern is not the inheritance itself but our relationship with God, for if that is not right, there will be no eternal inheritance for us. What an appalling thought that any should deceive themselves on so important an issue! To God we must come; to God we *can* come, for his throne is a throne of grace, at the right hand of which is our great High Priest who has done everything to give his believing people the full right of access (4:14-16).

The writer of the letter to the Hebrews has brought the concept of the Sabbath to its climax. Rest and restoration are here. In one masterly argument he has shown that there has been only one true rest which God has had in view from the beginning. It was lost in Adam; it is recovered in Christ.

Just as the children of those who came out of Egypt could have said, 'We are going in…', though they were not yet there, on the basis of their faith in the promise of God to take them into Canaan, so believers in the Lord Jesus can say, 'We do enter…,' even though they, too, are not there yet. How do we know? Because Jesus, the captain of our salvation (2:10), *has* entered. He *is* there, and he has gone to prepare a place for us (John 14:2-3). We *are* entering, because he *has* entered. We make every effort to enter his rest (Hebrews 4:11) not because of its uncertainty but because of its importance. Striving toward heaven is the characteristic of a healthy Christian, because seeking God is the characteristic of a healthy Christian, and the Sabbath-rest which is the goal will be in evidence in the keeping of the Fourth Commandment which provides a rest which is a true foretaste of what believers will enjoy fully in eternity.

The writer to the Hebrews, then, sees Jesus, the Lord of the Sabbath, as having entered into his rest. The first Adam, the federal head of the whole human race, forfeited it, and his descendants forfeited it in him; the last Adam, the head of the church, has secured it, and all his children enter it in him. We have not entered that rest yet, for our fellowship with God is as yet only partial and imperfect, however blissful at times it may be to us. But Jesus has entered, for he is now seated at his Father's right hand, his work completed, and he has promised that he will bring his people to glory to be with him. Then will be the restoration of all things, and our relationship with God will be all that it ought to be, all that God intended it should be. We owe it all, says the writer, to Jesus, our Great High Priest who brings us into his Father's presence, perfect and complete in him.

On the seventh day God ceased (in the sense of having completed it) from his work of creation. Likewise, on the first day of the week Christ Jesus rose triumphant from the grave and entered his rest, having ceased from (in the same sense of his having completed it) his work of redemption. The writer to the Hebrews is at pains to emphasise throughout his letter, piling argument upon argument, the fact that Jesus has *completed* the work of redemption he came into this world to accomplish. In the introduction at 1:3 we read that 'when he had by himself purged our sins', he '*sat down* at the right hand of the Majesty on high'. His session at God's right hand denotes his cessation, his *rest*, on account of all having been accomplished. 'Finished!' he cried upon the cross as he gave up his spirit to his Father, and thence it was from the cross to the crown, to his heavenly seat, to bear the name which is above every name (Philippians 2:9), the firstborn from the dead as well as the firstborn over all creation, thereby having the pre-eminence (Colossians 1:15,18), now sitting at the right hand of God his Father (Colossians 3:1; Ephesians 1:20; 1 Peter 3:22).

Note the way the Scriptures—for example Hebrews 10:12—speak of the finality and comprehensiveness of the redemptive work of Christ, and how the inspired writer deliberately uses the word 'sabbatismos' (4:9) for this. What he is telling us is this: that in the same way as God rested from his work of creation and blessed the seventh day (Genesis 2:3) (later interpreted as the Sabbath—Exodus 20:11), in the same way as he blessed the day to man in the bliss of his unfallen state, to enjoy the privilege of fellowship with his Creator, so Jesus has rested from his work of redemption and blessed the Sabbath rest to his redeemed people to enjoy the unspeakable privilege of fellowship with his Redeemer. It is essentially the *same* Sabbath-rest spoken of throughout.

Now *that* is the rest which we are exhorted to make every effort to enter into (4:11), which is specifically called a 'sabbatismos'—a Sabbath rest—at 4:9. As far as I can see this can have but one meaning. What man irretrievably lost by disobedience in Adam has been recovered in Christ. Now, though, it has a gloriously enlarged dimension, because added to the wonder of creation is the even greater wonder of redemption. Those who live in the nature of their fallen forefather are quite at a loss to understand the significance of this fourth of the Ten Commandments and its relation to the previous three, because they live at enmity with their Creator. Those to whom the Law was given who persisted in unbelief demonstrated their unbelief by disobedience, at every point failing to enter into the rest God promised those who would believe in him. They despised the Sabbath, as is indicated in passages like Amos 8:5; Isaiah 58:13-14; Jeremiah 17:21-27; Ezekiel 20:13,16,19-21; Nehemiah 13:15-22—passages we have already looked into and which, as we have seen, have much to say about the true intended purpose of the Sabbath. But what Adam lost Christ has regained, and although we have not actually yet entered into it, he has; and although for those who persist in unbelief it is gone for ever, for those who believe it remains, and the way we demonstrate this central truth is by seeking to keep the Sabbath now, our God setting his seal to it by graciously revealing himself to us as we meet to seek his face, and giving us a foretaste of what is yet to be enjoyed in full communion with him.

The Sabbath-rest therefore refers not to heaven itself, but to the complete restoration of the right relationship with God which will find its fulfilment in 'the new heavens and a new earth in which righteousness dwells' (2 Peter 3:13). Christians who are longingly looking for this fulfilment of God's promise will place a correspondingly high value on the Sabbath of the Fourth Commandment, nurturing the desire that the foretaste may soon become the real thing.

The Lord's Day

In the foregoing, to put it negatively, nothing has been found throughout the Scriptures, though they have been carefully examined, to suggest that the Fourth Commandment has ceased to apply or to be relevant to the Christian church, or that in the gospel age it is a thing of the past.[8] On the contrary, in looking carefully into what it is all about, it should have become increasingly apparent that it is of fundamental importance to the believer, its meaning and relevance shining that much more brightly in the light of the finished work of Christ. While there remains a Sabbath-rest for the people of God, in its essential nature the same as the Sabbath-rest we met in Genesis, let them pursue it with eagerness, honouring him on his day. In this chapter we shall briefly examine why the day, *his* day, has been transferred from Saturday to Sunday, from the seventh day to the first day. In case it is not obvious to anyone, the transference is not back six days, but forward one day. That is, there is a distinct movement *forward* in time from the 'old' Sabbath to the 'new'.

Some people are troubled by the fact that the New Testament letters appear to give no command about Sabbath-keeping. However, it is equally true that they are packed with guidance for the conduct of the gathered church which is totally consistent with what we have learnt about the Sabbath from the studies of the foregoing chapters. Furthermore, the New Testament church in the early days had only the Old Testament and such Gospels and apostolic letters as were then in circulation, and this comprised the basis of their teaching which it was not necessary to repeat. There is a regrettable tendency in some quarters of the church today (as was observed in an earlier chapter) to make a dichotomy between the Old and New Testaments as if the New supersedes the Old, instead of thinking in terms of continuity and development so that the New casts further light on the meaning of the Old. The New Testament both quotes from, and alludes so extensively to, the Old, and in such a variety of ways, that it should be clear that what is found there is authoritative. The apostles in their writings made very clear where some aspects of the law given through Moses no longer applied to the church because of the manner of their fulfilment in Christ. Then why was nothing said by them which hinted at any modification in the Ten Commandments? Whenever there is any New Testament reference to any of the Ten Commandments it is only in recognition of their continuing relevance and application. The New Testament writers neither repeat nor rewrite the Ten Commandments, for the simple reason that they stand as they are, needing neither repeating nor rewriting. Rather, they refer to them in the glorious light of the full revelation of the gospel, in which light we see what they mean in a manner we could only relatively dimly make out before. Thus the rich teaching about the Sabbath which is found in the pages of the Old Testament is given greater depth and colour when we view it through the eyes of New Testament teaching.

The Sabbath rest originally instituted by God came after creation's work had been completed, and in a sense was a commemoration of all God's works, which man would celebrate in fellowship with his Maker. This was lost through sin, but recovered through the redemptive work of Christ. This work of redemption followed on from the work of creation, and just as the 'old' Sabbath came at the end of what had been accomplished in creation, so the 'new' Sabbath comes at the end of the accomplishment of redemption. Jesus burst forth from the grave in resurrection glory early on the first day of the week, after the Sabbath was over. So in a sense it is not only fitting, it is also entirely consistent with the principle upon which God established his rest for man to enter into. Our commemoration and celebration rest upon salvation accomplished, not salvation foreshadowed. The finished works of God for the believer encompass not just creation, but creation and salvation. The transference from the old to the new is logical, meaningful, and appropriate.

This is all very well, but what do the Scriptures themselves indicate? It may surprise some readers to learn that the term 'The Lord's Day', which is used extensively in the Christian church for Sunday, is found in only one place in the Bible, namely in Revelation 1:10, when John said, 'I was in the Spirit on the Lord's Day'. Though John does not explicitly say he means the first day of the week, there can be little doubt that this is the case, as we shall see.

I have sought to demonstrate from the Bible that God has established the Sabbath as the day of blessing for man, the day he has sanctified, and that there is nothing inherently sacred about the seventh day *as the seventh day*, but that it was the day denoting cessation from work, the day denoting the completion of God's work, the day which he set apart for man. Throughout the Old Testament the Sabbath was the seventh day, for at that time there was nothing to supersede the pattern established at creation. It is interesting, though, that in the prophetic ceremonial law there were hints at the coming blessing accruing to the day *following* the seventh day Sabbath, and I will briefly make some observations about these next.

In Leviticus 23:10-11 we read that the sheaf of the firstfruits of the harvest in the land of promise was to be waved on the day after the Sabbath (at the time of the Passover—see also Joshua 5:10-12). This was the 'feast of firstfruits'. Seven weeks later, again on the day after the Sabbath, there was to be the offering of the wave loaves, interestingly baked with yeast, described as firstfruits to the Lord (verses 15-17). This latter day was called the 'feast of weeks', and was decreed as a holy convocation on which no work was to be done (verse 21). In other words, though the day after the Sabbath, it was the equivalent of a Sabbath. The parallels of these two events with the resurrection of Christ and Pentecost are unmistakable, and as the Old Testament ceremonial laws were prophetic in their import we are intended to take note of the connection.

For the Israelites in the wilderness a time interval of forty years was interposed between the first Passover and the feast of firstfruits, a sober reminder of what they had forfeited through unbelief. The sheaf of firstfruits waved on the day after the Sabbath would have been that of barley, which was the first to ripen. The firstfruits offering was not to be burned on the altar (Leviticus 2:12-14), probably because it spoke of Christ, 'the firstfruits of those who have fallen asleep' (1 Corinthians 15:20), after his work of suffering was over. *First*-fruits, by its very name, betokens a harvest: it is the guarantee of all that is to follow. *His* resurrection is the guarantee of the resurrection of all those who are his. The firstfruits is a foretaste of what is to come. That is why Christians should have their sights set firmly on the fulfilment of all the promises.

We are probably more familiar with the Greek name, 'Pentecost' for the

Feast of Weeks. The reference, as has been observed, is to what took place fifty days after the Passover Sabbath, or seven weeks from the offering of sheaf of the firstfruits. The harvest of barley was by now over, but not yet that of other cereals: the early harvest was giving way to a fuller one. Again, this took place on the *first* day of the week. On this occasion there were '*two* wave loaves', they were to be baked with yeast, and they are described as the '*firstfruits* to the Lord' (verse 17). Thus by the use of the same term, 'firstfruits', by the marking off of this complete period of time of *seven* weeks, and by the description of a '*new* grain offering to the Lord' (verse 16), this event is directly linked with the Feast of Firstfruits. Add to this the reference to 'the poor' and 'the stranger' (or foreigner) (verse 22), and the whole seems to point in one direction only: the beginning of a great harvest of souls arising from Christ *the* firstfruits (the word is used in this connection in Romans 8:23; 16:5; Revelation 14:4). There were 'two' wave loaves, not seven, probably because it represented a beginning; they were baked 'with leaven', perhaps because they represented saved sinners, not Christ; and it was a 'new' grain offering because in kind it was totally unlike anything which had preceded it. It is connected with a harvest which included not only the Jews, but the 'poor', and the 'stranger'—an undoubted reference to Gentiles who had come to hope in the God of Israel. It was from Jerusalem at Pentecost (Acts 2:1) that the gospel began to go out to 'all Judea and Samaria, and to the end of the earth' (Acts 1:8).

It could also be noted that the full range of accompanying offerings is here, headed up by *seven* lambs as a burnt offering (verses 18-20); and that it was at Pentecost, fifty days after the resurrection of our Lord Jesus Christ, that the *full* glories of his finished work of suffering upon the cross were first declared to the whole world.

Though we have skimmed the surface, the record stands, details heaped one upon another until the testimony is overwhelming: 'You were ... redeemed ... with the precious blood of Christ, as of a lamb without blemish and without spot. He indeed was foreordained before the foundation of the world, but was made manifest in these last times for you...' (1 Peter 1:18-21). The fruit of his work, firstly in his rising from the dead, and then in his resurrection life imparted to about three thousand people at Pentecost, was foretold, albeit in shadowy form, in the Old Testament law, as taking place in each case on the day after the Sabbath, on the first day of the week. Tying this in with the Sabbath rest procured by our Lord Jesus Christ, the testimony of the Old Testament law is that this is associated with the first day of the week, and so it is fitting that this should be considered the Christian Sabbath.

The early Christians indeed made a habit of meeting together on the first day of the week, the day of resurrection, and this was viewed independently of the seventh day Sabbath. Though historically there came to be an equating of 'the Lord's Day' with 'the Sabbath', this was not simply the development of a tradition, for it was authenticated by the Lord himself. We have already noted the prophetic testimony of the Old Testament. Now in the New Testament we should notice that there is an emphasis on the first day of the week which corresponds to the *purpose* of the Sabbath. To start with, it was the day of resurrection, and John (20:1,19) emphasises that it was the first day of the week, the day of triumph denoting that redemption's work was *done, finished*. It was the day in which the Lord met with his disciples. Again, in John 20:26, we read, '… after *eight days* his disciples were again inside, and Thomas with them. Jesus came, the doors being shut, and stood in the midst, and said, 'Peace to you!'.' It should be explained that, as they included the first day in their counting, this was again the first day of the week. The Day of Pentecost (Acts 2:1), too, was the first day of the week, in which the New Testament church was visibly born, in which the Lord manifested his presence in power among his people.

Thus in all of these cases the Lord Jesus very clearly put his stamp upon the first day of the week. By Acts 20:7 it is clear that the first day of the week had become the day in which the Lord's people met to remember him in the breaking of bread, a day of fellowship with him and with one another, and this practice of the church meeting on the first day of the week is confirmed in 1 Corinthians 16:2.

Furthermore, it was on what was called 'the Lord's Day' that John had his vision of the risen Christ (Revelation 1:10). What is this day which is so described? We are not told that this was the first day of the week, neither is this description used anywhere else in the Bible (except that the same construction in Greek is used in 1 Corinthians 11:20 where Paul writes of 'the Lord's supper'). However, the very fact that he writes in this way seems to indicate a particular day, one which is uniquely associated with the Lord, *and one which would be understood by his readers*. It is '*the Lord's* Day'. That is to say, the Lord has put his imprimatur upon it by declaring it to be *his* day. The first day of the week is *his* day. It is *for him*. And yet clearly at the same time it is for his people. In every way this corresponds exactly with the Sabbath, which God had called 'my holy day' (Isaiah 58:13), except that it has a far more glorious aspect than the seventh day Sabbath could ever have had because here we experience fellowship *restored*, here we recognize the riches of God's love toward us in Christ, here we confess with wonder that it is all of grace.

For Christians, I believe the Bible is indicating that what John describes as the Lord's Day is our Sabbath. In Christ we have had restored to us the enjoyment of a privilege which was lost when Adam sinned. This is to be our day of special fellowship with our Maker and our Redeemer. This fellowship may be very partial, very imperfect, and there may be many hindrances to it; but we remember, we observe, the Sabbath day to keep it holy in anticipation of the best which is yet to come, declaring to the world that to be with Christ is our hope, our joy and our ambition.

Conclusions

What I have endeavoured to do is to look at the great fundamentals of the Sabbath and why it was enshrined in the law of Ten Commandments. Its place was upheld by Jesus the Redeemer, and its observance is meaningful in the context of the redemption which is in Christ.

As we have studied the subject we have seen that all passages referring to the Sabbath say essentially the same thing of it, all speak with the same voice and use the same language. What we read in Hebrews is fully consistent with the teaching of Genesis; what Jesus said of the Sabbath is exactly what the prophets contended for in their time. The Sabbath remains, an inviolable testimony to the grace of God who purposed in Christ to bring his believing people back into the blessing of it. Jesus having entered his rest, what greater incentive do we need to remember the Sabbath, to keep it holy?

Perhaps some of you can remember courting days, and having to work during the week, all the time looking forward to the weekend because you could spend it with the one you loved. You had an appointment to keep with one another which was sacrosanct—you know what that word means—sacred and sanctified—inviolable—and woe betide anyone or anything which threatened to interfere with the arrangement! That appointment was so that you could spend as much time together as possible, to get to know one another better, to give your love the chance to deepen and mature. Let me challenge you now in regard to the Sabbath, which certainly was, and I maintain still is, God's sacrosanct appointment with his people. God hasn't changed, nor has his intended purpose for men and women changed. His creation ordinances, of which the Sabbath is one, still apply. If indeed there is any coolness on our part in our prospect of this appointment, the change is entirely in us. In giving us the day, God has promised to draw near to us as we draw near to him. I do believe as Christians we need really to get hold of this amazing and precious truth, for it seems to me that the very essence of the Sabbath has somehow been lost among all the intellectual baggage we carry around with us in regard to the purpose of the Sabbath and the practicalities of how the day should be spent.

By their disobedience toward God and the entry of sin into the world, our progenitors Adam and Eve severed fellowship with their Maker and thereby destroyed the intended blessing of the Sabbath rest. If our view of the Sabbath is indifferent, or cool, or cold, it is simply on account of our own personal sinfulness. Suppose we call a spade a spade. There is no point in hedging round the issue. Does our view of the Sabbath fall short of God's intended purpose? Either it does or it doesn't. The reason may have been on account of ignorance, or it may be because of unbelief. But whatever the reason, the problem is entirely our own, and we need in God's presence humbly to admit it. If this is the case, what we are admitting to is this: that *we are not entering into God's rest as we ought.* Yet, as we have seen, a promise remains of entering his rest (Hebrews 4:1). Though we seem so devastatingly to have undermined God's highest purpose for us, yet he has given us a promise of restoration.

Much of the problem Christians have with the law is when they view it legalistically, in terms of 'dos and don'ts', and this would apply especially to the Sabbath. God never intended legalistic observance, but spiritual obedience. This is not lesser obedience, but proper obedience, holy obedience. So when it comes to Sabbath-keeping, we keep it in the spirit, with an understanding of its intended purpose, and in anticipation of what is yet to be, which we by grace have begun to enter into, but the complete enjoyment of which is eagerly awaited.

Where motivation exists, method will follow, and a way will be found to honour the Lord on his day. There are countless instances of people who have compromised on keeping Sunday for the Lord and suffered spiritually as a consequence. For those in service industries where some Sunday work is a necessity (such as the medical profession, to name an obvious one) there will often be an ongoing struggle to maintain a distinction between what must be done and what need not be done, that is, to maintain the distinction between works of necessity associated with the profession, and all the other things which tend to be 'built into' the system by those who make no distinction between the days.

Our purpose has not been to lay down rules and regulations about how the Lord's Day should be spent, but to highlight principles from the Word of God which can be worked out in whatever circumstances the reader may be found. Because the Sabbath had a special place in the nation of Israel's constitution, it made it relatively easy for people to keep it, at least in the strict outward sense of doing no work on the day. When there was national degeneration, however, things became much more difficult. One of the differences between the Fourth Commandment and the first three is that it has more of a public face to it and its observance requires a measure of cooperation from society. For all the blessings pertaining to the Lord's Day, keeping it will often accentuate the fact that we live in a hostile world and remind us that we have not yet entered God's rest in the fullest sense. That is yet to come, and is attained by faith.

Of course there are difficulties in keeping the Sabbath in our own generation, as indeed there have been throughout history, but this is no reason for capitulating to the pressures of the world and either compromising or giving up. In our world we will suffer intrusions upon both our legitimate work and our legitimate rest. Both will be subjected to pressures, because we live in a world which is hostile to God and his laws. Very few readers will find themselves in the position of being unable to keep the Sabbath because of persecution of one form or another. If others prohibit or hinder our remembrance, the Lord will hold them accountable; but if *we* neglect it, he will hold us accountable. It is very unlikely that the apostle John's circumstances on Patmos were conducive to his remembering the Sabbath, banished as he was to the island because of his testimony to Christ (Revelation 1:9). Nevertheless, in spite of all that was against him, he was 'in the Spirit on the Lord's Day', making such use of the day as he could. In our diligent attempt to preserve our day of fellowship with God, as well as in our diligent attempt to do our work to the glory of God, we will maintain an effective witness to what it means to be the Lord's people. May we be enabled to live such lives among people that they may glorify God on the day of visitation. Indeed, may it please God to visit them in grace before the last great and terrible day of judgement.

So-called Sabbath observance has suffered much at the hands of legalists over the years. But that is not an argument to do away with it. Because a privilege is abused it may be taken away: but it is no less a privilege for that. Its removal is a loss to those who abuse it. Of those who maintain that the Sabbath of the Fourth Commandment is a thing of the past, some among them argue that every day for the New Testament believer is a Sabbath, and that we are to have fellowship with God all day every day. Again, with due respect to them, this is not what the Bible says, and they are confusing things which differ, which I have sought to show in these studies and need not repeat now. While it is right that we should be *in* fellowship with God at all times, it seems to me that those who say they can *have* fellowship with God as much in their work as they can in their rest are either not doing their work very well or not enjoying their fellowship with God very well!

Because we saw that the Sabbath was to be a sign (in the second chapter of this book), in case there is any misunderstanding it ought to be made clear that the Sabbath, or for us the Lord's Day, is not *primarily* for gospel witness. It is not a sign in that sense. Testimony to Christ will be the greater when we honour the Sabbath in his way. We must always work from biblical principles to practice. A pragmatic approach, such as 'My participation in the local football match on a Sunday will enable me to witness to the team' sounds fine in theory, but carries little weight. My not participating in the match, in spite of my love of the game and enthusiasm for it on any other day, will tell far more on the other members, and will be a far more effective witness to what it means to belong to Christ. To say, 'I am sacrificing my principles in order that I may speak with you about the Lord' deserves the rebuttal: 'You can't place a very high value on your principles!' Let's face it: if we have to make sacrifices in this world in respect of employment or leisure or pleasure because others use Sundays for these things when we want to use the day for the Lord, can we really harbour regrets? Isn't a day in the courts of the Lord (Psalm 84:10) more than compensation for all these things?

However much we may wish the society in which we live to 'keep Sunday special', and however much it grieves us to see the general disregard for God in so many ways, we have to recognize that those who are not Christians have no idea of what the Fourth Commandment is all about, and if they did they would still have no desire to observe it. In the very first chapter of this book the point was made from Exodus 20:10 that providing the rest which the Sabbath required so that others could benefit was the responsibility of the people of God. Later, when the Israelites were found trading on the Sabbath, as well as breaking the commandment themselves, they were actually hindering others from any benefit accruing to the Sabbath. They were responsible for causing or encouraging their servants, or their animals, or the foreigners who were among them, to work when God said they should be given rest, and so they compounded a bad testimony with action which was detrimental to the welfare of others. How we live out what God requires of us affects more than ourselves. We might wish others to keep Sunday special so that we can benefit, whereas really it should be the other way round. It is our responsibility to be keeping the Sabbath as God intended so that others might benefit. How we use the Lord's Day really does affect other people as well as ourselves.

This is far removed from seeking to impose the Sabbath on other people. God gave the Sabbath (as he did the rest of his commandments) to his covenant people, that through their sphere of influence it might reach out and embrace others. Remember that by 'covenant people' we understand those who have entered into covenant with God to obey all that he requires. Non-Christians have not entered into covenant with God. They have not said they will either obey God or serve him. The answer to the question whether Christians have responsibility to impose any of God's commandments on others hinges upon the extent of their sphere of influence and authority. This is no place for a detailed discussion of this point. What we need to bear in mind is simply that we are to set an example of godliness in this world, seeking by all legitimate means to bring others into the blessings God in love bestows through his Son. Our sphere of influence will in most cases include our immediate family, and our church family, and perhaps in some cases, say for Christians with leadership responsibilities in their professions, it may extend to business life. As a general principle observable from the Word of God, whenever God's people walk closely with him, he is pleased for the sake of the gospel to extend their sphere of influence. The key to it all is our walk with God. Our walk with God is most in evidence in our use of the Lord's Day.

Blessed be God for the Sabbath! 'It is good to give thanks to the LORD, and to sing praises to your name, O Most High; to declare your lovingkindness in the morning, and your faithfulness every night' (Psalm 92:1-2. The Sabbath is a day of special privilege in which we can meditate upon the works and ways of God in a manner which is not possible when our minds are engaged upon our legitimate work. But then also our time with the Lord on his day prepares us for the work we do during the week. Our time spent with him gives meaning and purpose to our daily work. Christians should not suffer from the proverbial 'Monday morning blues'. Indeed, our attitude should be quite the opposite.

It has not been my purpose in these studies to say what should or should not be done on the Sabbath, or the Lord's Day. This would savour of legalism. We cannot legislate for fellowship with God, but we can at least do what we can to eliminate man-made hindrances to that fellowship. If we understand what the Bible teaches about the Sabbath, and have got a firm hold of the principles, then we may look to the Lord for help with their outworking. Practical ways to use the Lord's Day well should have occurred to the reader in the course of the study of these pages. Certainly meeting with God's people, certainly speaking of him, certainly seeking to draw others into sincere worship of the Lord, certainly hearing and pondering his Word; certainly in doing good to others for his sake as there is opportunity. There may be place for relaxation, for resting, for recuperating from the demands of a busy week; yet these are not the things which were ever principally in view in the Sabbath. The real refreshment is that which we experience as we sit at the Master's feet, as we enjoy his presence and hear his voice. It would not be difficult to produce a long list of suggestions for the improvement of our use of the Lord's Day. After what has been written, though, we dare not reduce it to a list of sanctions and prohibitions.[9] If we properly understand the Sabbath-rest, our hearts should be burning with desire to improve our relationship with him, to be more intimate with him, to know him better, to walk in fellowship with him.

God has promised to draw near to those who draw near to him (James 4:8). This very particularly applies on the Lord's Day. Until the personal return of our Lord Jesus Christ his appointed way of speaking to us is through his Word and in particular its public proclamation on his day. We meet together to meet with him; we grow in the grace and knowledge of our Lord Jesus Christ (2 Peter 3:18) as we receive and understand his Word. It is the church which is the bride of Christ, which is the body of Christ, and individually we are only members. It is as a body that we should recognize our belonging to him, that we find our highest fulfilment in fellowship with him. Therefore every activity of the church which takes place on the Lord's Day should be directed to the promotion of that end. He himself has given us all we need in this respect, for 'He himself gave some to be apostles, some prophets, some evangelists, and some pastors and teachers, for the equipping of the saints for the work of ministry, for the edifying of the body of Christ, till we all come to the unity of the faith and of the knowledge of the Son of God, to a perfect man, to the measure of the stature of the fullness of Christ' (Ephesians 4:11-13).

May God help us to understand the great principle of the Sabbath, and to work it out here below in preparation for that time when we shall observe it in the new heavens and the new earth, the home of righteousness (2 Peter 3:13).

Notes

1. **Reisinger, Ernest C.,** *Whatever Happened to the Ten Commandments?* The Banner of Truth Trust, 1999, p.46.

2. **Edwards, Brian H.,** *The Ten Commandments for Today*, Day One Publications, 2002. An excellent, relevant and eminently readable treatment of the law, scholarly and incisive. Edwards writes cogently on what I have scantily treated in chapter 3.

3. See, for example, **Bayes, Jonathan F.,** *The threefold division of the law*, The Christian Institute, 2005. In this booklet Bayes argues that although the words 'moral', 'civil' and 'ceremonial' are theological terms, it is apparent that they do justice to vital scriptural distinctions. The article was reprinted from one which first appeared in 'Reformation Today', Issue 177. Bayes briefly traces the history of this threefold division, showing that it was recognized at least from the time of Augustine in the 5th Century.

4. Appeal has sometimes been made to the fact that many among the Reformers regarded the Sabbath as a ceremonial law. However, Fairbairn, in an appendix to *The Typology of Scripture* (see the bibliography for details) points out that the Reformers generally, in their view of the Sabbath, appeared to be influenced by the ecclesiastical background from which they had emerged and against which they had justly reacted, cluttered as it was with rites and ceremonies. Thus, doubtless without intending it, their interpretation at this point may have been guided more by prejudice than by careful analysis of the Scriptures, and the little that they wrote on this subject seems to support the suggestion. Calvin, for example, is sometimes quoted as one who regarded the Fourth Commandment as being a ceremonial law and therefore not applicable to the Christian church. A bald statement like this, though, is hardly a just representation of his position, and a thorough reading of what he wrote on the subject casts it in a very different light. His discourses to the church in Geneva indicate that he had a clear appreciation of the principle of the Sabbath in its positive aspect

relating to the worship of God, while his practice accordingly followed the course of a heart devoted to God.

Dabney, writing with his customary pithy clarity (*Discussions: Evangelical and Theological*, Volume 1, pages 496-550), picks up on the division of opinion among the Reformers concerning the perpetuity of the Fourth Commandment, lamenting the fact that this has been inherited by subsequent generations of Christians, many of whom have simply held to one position or the other without making the effort of an honest examination of the biblical teaching on the subject. It would be fair to say that this position pertains today in the United Kingdom. For many Christians, not only is there great ignorance of what the Fourth Commandment teaches, there is also a general lack of concern to understand its meaning and relevance. It is almost as if a large part of the Christian church is keeping its eyes shut lest the light should hurt.

5. I do not consider there is any substance to the suggestion made by some that the title to the psalm is not part of the inspired text.

6. Many authors refer in some form or another to the rest which believers enjoy in Christ, clearly alluding to Hebrews 4, yet base their arguments on an assumption about what that chapter is saying rather than on careful exegesis. It is for this reason that a correct understanding of this chapter is so important.

7. In his massive commentary on the Epistle to the Hebrews, John Owen frequently asserts that the Sabbath is a pledge of our rest in God, and also in one place at least that it is a pledge of the recovery of this rest for us (Vol.4, p.324). He argues that while most expositors of his and previous times applied verse 10 of chapter 4 to believers, he was convinced it referred to Christ. Having deliberately produced most of this book without reference to commentaries, turning to them only after long study of the Scriptures on this subject, it was a great encouragement to me, in the face of the contrary interpretation of many more recent expositors, to discover that Owen held the same view as me of this verse. While not agreeing with him completely in the analysis of this section of Hebrews, I would heartily recommend the work to anyone prepared to give time to it, for such a study is potentially immensely

rewarding. Owen is meticulously thorough and careful, a master whose every thought committed to paper has first been submitted to the scrutiny of the Word of God, as he has compared Scripture with Scripture in his pursuit of a clear and rounded understanding of the text and argument.

Owen says, in his introduction to Hebrews 4, that 'the 'rest' which the psalmist speaks of, and which he persuades them to endeavour an entrance into … [is] neither the rest of God from the works of creation, with the sabbatical rest which ensued thereon, verses 4-6; nor yet the rest of Canaan, which Joshua brought the people into, verses 7, 8; but a spiritual rest, which remained for believers to enjoy, verses 8-10' (Vol.4, p.198). He enlarges on his meaning (p.274) with reference to what he calls 'the *threefold state of the church* of God under consideration:– (1.) The state of it under *the law of nature* or creation; (2.) The state of it under *the law of institutions* and carnal ordinances; (3.) That now introducing *under the gospel*. To each of these he [that is, the writer of the Letter to the Hebrews] assigns a distinct rest of God, a rest of the church entering into God's rest, and a day of rest as a means and pledge thereof. And withal he manifests that the former two were ordered to be previous representations of the latter, though not equally nor on the same account.' A little later (p.277) Owen admits that the context is involved and observes that the commentators of his day had shed very little light on it.

While agreeing in broad outline with Owen's thesis, I maintain that, more than a common thread running through each of the 'rests' so described, there is an essential unity in them; indeed, that only one rest is really being spoken of. The rest which was forfeited by man at the beginning through his rejection of God's word is recovered for him through the obedience and sacrifice of Christ for those who will now accept his word in the gospel. The 'rest' of the Sabbath of the Fourth Commandment, and the 'rest' of Canaan, were provided by God for his people that they might enjoy and benefit from a foretaste of the spiritual rest which is to be found in Christ alone, and only in the new heaven and new earth. They were not only prophetic of the true rest, they were also real and substantial provisions for the people of God to prepare them for what was promised. The true 'rest', says the writer to the Hebrews, was *given* not at creation (for man lost it), nor in the law given through Moses, nor in the land of inheritance under the leadership of Joshua: it was given by Christ, and is to be entered into through faith in him. All Christians know, as long as they have to contend against the world, the flesh and the devil, that they have not yet entered into their rest. What they do know is that Jesus has entered on their behalf, and will bring them into the good of it. Therefore they strive to enter. I maintain that one of the principal manifestations of this striving is to be seen in the right honouring of the Fourth Commandment. There is a difference between *not* entering God's rest as a result of his judgement, and not *yet* having entered.

There is a remarkable statement in Hebrews 11:13, of the many who died in faith, not having received the promises. At first sight it reads as if it were the ultimate tragedy: they died without receiving what was promised. They had lived with it in view, forsaking the pleasures of this world in order to pursue what was promised, but died before receiving it. What wasted effort! What bitter disappointment! And so it would have been but for one thing: they were 'seeking a homeland', desiring 'a better, that is, a heavenly country' (11:14,16). That they did not receive the promises in this life was of little consequence to them, for they were looking to receiving them in the resurrection. So, similarly, the believer does not enter into God's rest in this life, but is nevertheless making every effort to enter it (4:11), knowing that an entrance into the everlasting kingdom of his Lord and Saviour Jesus Christ will be abundantly supplied (2 Peter 1:10,11). The Christian, *in this life*, is ever reaching forward to what cannot be attained or obtained in this life. This is not nonsense. The reason for it is that he or she has a new nature and is indwelt by the Spirit of God, and therefore belongs not to this world but to that which is to come. Hence there is a yearning to live according to the life of heaven. Because we are going there, we are already endeavouring to live according to the 'rules' of heaven, and how better than by grasping every opportunity with both hands to improve our acquaintance with the One whom we shall shortly worship throughout eternity.

8. This is not to ignore what has been said on the other side of the debate. In 1982 Zondervan published a work edited by Don Carson entitled *From Sabbath to Lord's Day: A Biblical, Historical and Theological Investigation*. A review which appeared in The Journal of the Evangelical Theological Society in 1984 commences: 'This book has become something of a classic representative of the 'Sunday is not the Sabbath' line of interpretation.' A number of summaries

and reviews have been posted on the web and may be found by entering the book title in the search field.

It is a scholarly and meticulous presentation which runs counter to what I have presented in these pages. If it seems strange that I should draw attention to such a work, it is simply in confirmation of what I said at the outset, that it is vital that we should reach conclusions firmly anchored in the bedrock of Scripture. Having compared Scripture with Scripture, any interpretation we present on this subject must be consistent with the *whole* of the Word of God. Furthermore, this consistency must include not only the matter directly under consideration, but all other areas on which it directly or indirectly impinges. One test of whether our interpretation is right will be when it provides us with clear answers to those who hold a different view.

It is a curious fact that among those who hold a cessationist view of the Sabbath, many are still so concerned to maintain a 'one day in seven' principle for meeting and worship that they have to find reasons largely outside of Scripture for doing so! It is surprising that they should not think this alarming. Even more alarming, though, is that they should be satisfied that only tenuous arguments from the Bible remain in support of their position.

9. I am not suggesting there is no place for guidelines on how to use the Lord's Day or that those who have provided such advice are being in any way legalistic. Stuart Olyott, in 'The Right Use of the Lord's Day' (*Day One* Magazine, October '05—January '06), comments pithily: 'Those who find Sunday 'boring' are nearly always people who have become self-centred.' This is a brief article highlighting what he calls eleven facts concerning the Sabbath, followed by indications of what we should not do and what we should do on Sundays. Others have gone into much greater detail on how Sundays are to be used by Christians. However, in keeping with the purpose of this book, I want the reader to work out practice from his or her own understanding of what the Scriptures teach on the subject.

Bibliography

Bayes, Jonathan F., *The threefold division of the law*, The Christian Institute, 2005.

Campbell, Iain D., *On the first day of the week*, Day One, 2005.

Carson, D. A., ed., *From Sabbath to Lord's Day: A Biblical, Historical and Theological Investigation*, Zondervan, 1982.

Chantry, Walter J., *Call The Sabbath a Delight*, The Banner of Truth Trust, 1991.

Dabney, Robert Lewis, 'The Christian Sabbath: Its Nature, Design and Proper Observance.' *Discussions: Evangelical and Theological*, The Banner of Truth Trust, Volume 1, 1982, pages 496-550.

Edwards, Brian H., *The Ten Commandments for Today*, Day One, 2002.

Edwards, Jonathan, 'The Perpetuity and Change of the Sabbath.' *The Works of Jonathan Edwards*, The Banner of Truth Trust, Volume 2, 1974, pages 93-103.

Fairbairn, Patrick, 'Appendix A: Views of the Reformers regarding the Sabbath.' *The Typology of Scripture*, Evangelical Press, 1975, pages 447-459.

Hulse, Erroll, 'Sanctifying the Lord's Day: Reformed and Puritan Attitudes.' Westminster Conference, 1981, page 78.

Lee, Nigel, *The Covenantal Sabbath*, The Lord's Day Observance Society, 1972.

Murray, John, 'The Moral Law and the Fourth Commandment.' *Collected Writings of John Murray*, The Banner of Truth Trust, Volume 1, 1976, pages 193-228.

Owen, John, *The Epistle to the Hebrews*, Evansville: Sovereign Grace, 1960.

Pipa, Joseph A., *The Lord's Day*, Christian Focus, 1997.

Reisinger, Ernest C., *Whatever Happened to the Ten Commandments?* The Banner of Truth Trust, 1999.

Tow, Timothy, 'Jesus and the Dispensational View of the Sabbath. *The Law of Moses & of Jesus*, Christian Life Publishers, 1986, pages 115-123.

Warfield, B. B., 'The Foundations of the Sabbath in the Word of God.' *Selected Shorter Writings of B B Warfield*, Volume 2, Presbyterian and Reformed Publishing Company, 1973.

The Ten Commandments for today
Brian H Edwards

A modern commentary which carefully uncovers the true meaning of the Ten Commandments, and incisively applies them to our contemporary society.

'Edwards' book finds a well deserved place at the cutting edge of application of this important theme.'
THE BANNER OF TRUTH MAGAZINE

304pp, paperback, £9
ISBN 978-1-903087-33-6
REF: 10T 333

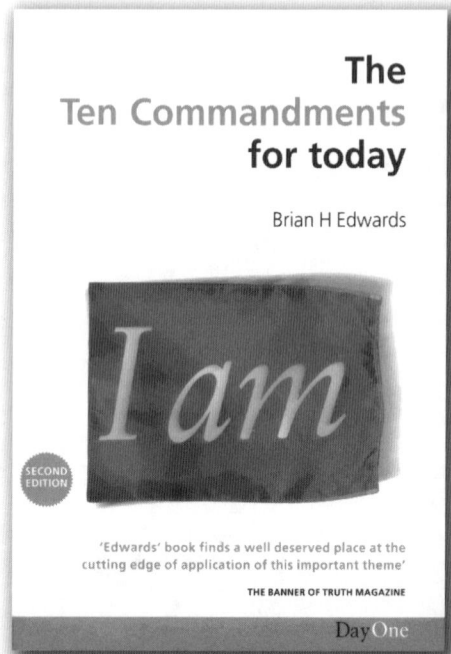

**The
Ten Commandments
for today**

Brian H Edwards

I am

SECOND
EDITION

'Edwards' book finds a well deserved place at the
cutting edge of application of this important theme'

THE BANNER OF TRUTH MAGAZINE

Day One

On the first day of the week
God, the Christian and the Sabbath

Iain D Campbell

In an increasingly secular world, the personal and social benefits of Sabbath-keeping are being lost to us more and more. It is increasingly difficult to defend the traditional view that the fourth commandment is still binding on us, and that God wants us to honour the first day of the week, the Lord's Day, as a Christian Sabbath. This book examines some of the issues raised in this debate, and argues that for the Christian believer, the Sabbath principle is one which is still binding, relevant, necessary and beneficial.

Rev Dr Iain D Campbell is pastor of Back Free Church of Scotland on the Isle of Lewis. He contributes regularly to several theological journals. His wife, Anne, is a teacher, and they have three children.

'Dr Campbell's book is a joy to read. It is well written and easy to understand.'
JOEL BEEKE

224pp paperback, £8
ISBN 978-1-903087-95-4
REF: FDTW 953

IAIN D CAMPBELL

On the first day of the week
God, the Christian and the Sabbath

DayOne